Taking Your Soul to Work

Taking Your Soul to Work

Overcoming the Nine Deadly Sins
of the Workplace

R. Paul Stevens and Alvin Ung

William B. Eerdmans Publishing Company
Grand Rapids, Michigan / Cambridge, U.K.

© 2010 R. Paul Stevens and Alvin Ung
All rights reserved

Published 2010 by
Wm. B. Eerdmans Publishing Co.
2140 Oak Industrial Drive N.E., Grand Rapids, Michigan 49505 /
P.O. Box 163, Cambridge CB3 9PU U.K.
www.eerdmans.com

Printed in the United States of America

16 15 14 13 12 11 10   7 6 5 4 3 2 1

Library of Congress Cataloging-in-Publication Data

Stevens, R. Paul, 1937-
Taking your soul to work: overcoming the nine deadly sins of the workplace /
R. Paul Stevens and Alvin Ung.
p.   cm.
Includes bibliographical references and index.
ISBN 978-0-8028-6559-5 (pbk.: alk. paper)
1. Employees — Religious life. 2. Employees — Conduct of life.
I. Ung, Alvin, 1971-   II. Title.

BV4593.S74 2010

248.8'8 — dc22

2010020369

Contents

Contents

Foreword

One of the most offensive and soul-damaging phrases in the Christian community is "full-time Christian work." Every time it is used it drives a wedge of misunderstanding between the way we pray and the way we work, between the way we worship and the way we make a living. One of the achievements of the Protestant Reformation was a leveling of the ground between clergy and laity. Pastors and butchers had equal status before the cross. Homemakers were on a par with evangelists. But insidiously, that level ground has been eroded as religious professionals have claimed the high ground, asserted exclusive rights to "full-time Christian work," and relegated the laity to part-time work on weekends under their pastoral or priestly direction. The laity is demeaned with the adjectives "mere," "only," or "just": "he or she is *just* a layperson." This professionalization of religion is an assault on the integrity of the Christian community.

One of the encouraging developments in the Christian community in the last two or three decades is the emergence of men and women who are energetically reclaiming the witness and ministry of the laity, developing a passion, in the words of the writers of this book, to "take our souls to work."

Two things become apparent as this passion develops. One, the fences that have been erected between the language used in religion and the language used in work get knocked down. Language, all of it — every vowel, every consonant — is a gift of God.

God uses language to create and command us; we use language to confess our sins and sing praises to God. We use this very same language in getting to know one another, buying and selling, writing letters and reading books. We use the same words in talking to one another as we use when talking to God: the same nouns and verbs, adverbs and adjectives, conjunctions and interjections, prepositions and pronouns. There is no "Holy Ghost" language used for matters of God and salvation and then a separate secular language for buying cabbages and cars. "Give us this day our daily bread" and "pass the potatoes" come out of the same language pool.

God does not compartmentalize language into secular and religious, the world of work and the world of worship. Why do we? We are surrounded and blessed by many friends these days who are cultivating a continuity of language between the words we use in Bible studies and the words we use when we are out fishing for rainbow trout, the words we use when we are talking to or about God and the words we use when talking to our employers and employees about the stock market and business plans. We call all language sacred, a holy gift, regardless of whether it is directed vertically or horizontally. Just as Jesus did.

The element that comes into view as this passion "to take our souls to work" develops is a realization that most of what Jesus said and did took place in a secular setting, in a workplace: in a farmer's field, in a fishing boat, at a wedding feast, in a cemetery, at a public well asking a woman he didn't know for a drink of water, on a country hillside that he turned into a huge picnic, in a courtroom, at supper in homes with acquaintances or friends. In our Gospels, Jesus occasionally shows up in the synagogue or temple, but for the most part he spends his time in the workplace. Twenty-seven times in John's Gospel, Jesus is identified as a worker: "My Father is still working, and I also am working" (John 5:17). Work doesn't take us away from God; it continues the work of God. We observe that God comes into view on the first page of our Scripture as a worker, creating the universe. Once we identify God in his workplace working, it isn't long before we find ourselves in our workplaces working in the name of God.

If you are among the growing number of Christian men and women who want to take your souls into your workplace, this is the book for you. Paul Stevens and Alvin Ung have themselves been doing this for a long time on two continents, North America (Stevens) and Asia (Ung). They know firsthand what they are writing about. They are in the forefront of recovering the essential and rock-bottom necessity to provide informed direction for the laity, both men and women, who find themselves in the workplace as full-time Christian workers. They are wise guides. You can trust them. This is a major work for restoring dignity to the laity and infusing vigorous health into the Christian community.

EUGENE H. PETERSON
Professor Emeritus of Spiritual Theology
Regent College, Vancouver, B.C.

Introduction

A Conversation between the Authors

"My work's killing me," sighed Alvin, as he dipped his skewer of chicken satay into peanut sauce. "I simply don't have enough time during the day — and night — to get things done."

"You're in a tough spot," agreed Paul, as he watched the satay vendor grilling the skewered meat on a bed of red-hot coals. A heady mix of turmeric, lemongrass, and coriander filled the night air. "I've been in Kuala Lumpur for only two days but I can see that everyone's in a rush and working very long hours. Everywhere you go in the world, work has become so stressful — with increased competition, unrelenting job demands, and global financial turmoil. Companies are acting like headless chickens."

"I've heard of a chicken that lived for eighteen months with its head chopped off. That's me for the next three months," Alvin said. "Then I'll try to get my life back. Start swimming laps. Stop working weekends. Talk to my wife. Revive my prayer life."

"What happened to your prayer life?" Paul asked.

"My work suffocated it. I still believe in God and continue to go to church. But to be honest, for seventy hours a week or more, during the most productive hours of my day, I behave as if God doesn't exist," Alvin said, as he absent-mindedly stirred the satay sauce with a bamboo skewer. "Paul, do you really think it's possible to grow spiritually while I'm working in my crazy, relentless job?"

"Yes."

Alvin mused to himself. *How do I grow spiritually when I work?* That question had popped into his head unbidden. It sounded impossible. He was usually too stressed out during work to be conscious of God's presence. After work, he was too drained and brain-dead to pray. Work seemed to be a hindrance to, not a catalyst for, spiritual growth.

"I'd like to experience what it means to grow spiritually when I work," Alvin said. "Could you help me?"

"My dear friend, I may be older than you, but I'm no saint. Just like you, I face the external pressures of busyness and stress. But I'm painfully conscious of even greater pressures assaulting us from within — greed, anger, envy, pride, and much more. These things really hinder our spiritual growth in the workplace."

The conversation lapsed into silence as the twilight glow of the tropical sky got swallowed up by the encroaching darkness. The coals from the satay vendor glowed bright and hot.

"I have a proposal," Paul said. "Let's meet regularly to talk through and pray about how we can grow spiritually when we work."

"Given that I live and work in Malaysia, and you're in Canada, we'd have to do this by e-mail or telephone. And hopefully, once in a while, we could meet face-to-face," Alvin said.

"We can do that. And for a fruitful conversation, I think we'll need to address three things. First, we'll need to identify the soul-sapping struggles that are hindering us from growing spiritually while we work. This diagnostic work is tough but necessary. Next, we can reflect on how the Spirit of God enables us to work whole-heartedly. And third, we'll imagine the wonderful ways in which we can work differently with God's help," Paul said.

"Let's do it!" Alvin said.

How This Book Can Help You

Do you long for something more in your job than just making ends meet or climbing the corporate ladder? Do you yearn for the abiding presence of the Living God, energizing your thoughts, words, and actions while you work? Or do you wish to discern God's transforming work in *your* workplace and join God in fulfilling that agenda? Or maybe you simply have a sneaking suspicion that there's just got to be something more — something of greater value and meaning to work itself — than merely enduring a one-hour commute, surviving office politics, and pleasing your bosses and clients.

If you said yes to any of the above, we have written this book for you.

Like you, we long to take our souls to work, to be attentive to God's presence in the midst of a busy and intense work life, and to be gradually transformed into loving and holy persons while we work. These were our personal aspirations as we met for two years — in Bali, Kuala Lumpur, Vancouver, and other places — to pray and talk about what it means to grow spiritually in the workplace. At the same time, we brought different perspectives to our discussions because we come from different places, cultures, and work experiences.

Alvin Ung grew up in Malaysia and worked as a financial analyst, a foreign correspondent with the Associated Press, and a senior manager in the telecommunications industry before studying spiritual and marketplace theology at Regent College in Vancouver, British Columbia. He has subsequently managed a private foundation and worked as a senior executive in a Malaysian investment fund. Paul Stevens, a Canadian, has been a pastor, a carpenter, a business person, a professor of marketplace theology and leadership, and is now professor emeritus of marketplace theology at Regent College. He continues to teach and lecture in churches, theological schools, and companies.

We first met one another in a marketplace theology class taught by Paul. Over the years, we became friends as we co-taught classes, worked, and traveled together — constantly interacting with our Eastern and Western perspectives on work and life. Each of us is a "work in progress" on the journey of integrating faith and work, as you will see from our ongoing conversations.

We are followers of Jesus Christ. As such, our sensibilities, worldview, and writing are drawn from the rich tradition of Jewish and Christian Scriptures. At the same time, we hope that people of all faith traditions who are seeking a deeper workplace spirituality might find this book helpful. We've discovered few non-academic books that try to integrate work and spirituality. So, for this book, we've tapped the treasury of Christian spirituality — Roman Catholic, Protestant, and Orthodox — to help shed light on what it means to live as whole, integrated people in the workplace.

Alvin, who spent more than a decade working in Malaysia, a predominantly Muslim nation, has observed that the search for spirituality goes deep among his Muslim colleagues. A co-worker once told Alvin: "A Muslim is someone who's surrendered to God. This entails much more than outward acts of going to the mosque on Friday or praying five times a day. Being Muslim is more than counting the number of times we pray; it's learning to be prayerful when we are working. Tragically, among many Muslims today, there's a disconnect between our faith and our work. That's why corruption, injustice, and inequity remain entrenched in many Islamic countries. We would not behave in such a way if we were totally aware that Allah is with us in all things. Though I am far from this, I aspire to live this way."

As followers of Jesus, we, too, aspire to live this way — our lives surrendered to God, in prayerful union with Jesus, who is Ruler of the marketplace.

Reasons for a Spirituality of Work

Without having a deeper understanding of why we work, we find that life becomes bleached of meaning. We will feel stuck working in dead-end jobs that engage only a fraction of our gifts and aspirations. "When work is soulless, life stifles and dies," said the existentialist philosopher Albert Camus.[1]

Therefore a spirituality of work is necessary. Consciously or not, we are developing a spirituality of work when we agree with the following presuppositions:

4

- First, God is everywhere (including the workplace) and God loves everyone (including the worker).
- Second, we cannot do everything by ourselves. We depend on people; and we are especially dependent on God. While God has given us active roles in developing and growing ourselves, fundamentally we cannot do this without God.
- Therefore, third and most important, God actively seeks us out because he wants to continuously make us more like him while also making us more fully human. In this book, God's loving activity of seeking us out and transforming us is called the "fruit of the Spirit" (see Gal. 5:22).

While the term "spirituality" means many things to many people, we resonate most with Gregory Pierce's description of a spirituality of work as "a disciplined attempt to align ourselves and our environment with God and to be a concrete bodily expression of God's Spirit in the world through all the effort (paid and unpaid) we exert to make the world a better place, a little closer to the way God would have things."[2]

From Pierce's description, we draw three key movements in the spiritual life that help to describe a spirituality of work. We have organized this book around these three movements:

1. Identifying the struggles that prevent us from coming alive at work
2. Cultivating the Spirit of God who equips us with life-giving resources
3. Imagining the outcome of a Spirit-led life that welcomes God at the center of work

Identifying the Struggles In the first part of this book, we consider the ways in which soul-sapping struggles are deeply embedded in the life of the worker and the workplace. We have identified nine "deadly" sins that can easily entangle us as we work. Like weeds, these sins grow deep in our souls as well as within the culture, processes, and systems of the workplace; they must be rooted out continuously. We have included exercises that can help us in this challenging but invigorating process.

Cultivating the Spirit Next, we consider how God has given us nine life-giving resources to bring about transformation in our souls, as well in the organizations we work for. Each fruit of the Spirit (such as love, joy, peace, and so on) serves as a healing antidote to the soul-sapping struggles. We have included real-life examples of the Spirit's mighty work and have also suggested some spiritual disciplines for daily practice. Besides removing obstacles that could hinder us from knowing ourselves and knowing God, these disciplines help us become more receptive to God's work in our lives.

Imagining the Outcomes of a Spirit-Led Life Finally, we consider the results of workplace spirituality — what we get out of life and work when we welcome God into the center of all things. We have included thumbnail sketches of ordinary saints — people from all walks of life, past and present, from the East and West — whose lives embody the attributes we discuss.

How to Use this Book

The three parts of the book are clearly laid out in the matrix below.

Identifying the Soul–Sapping Struggles	Cultivating the Fruit of the Spirit	Imagining the Outcomes of a Spirit-Led Life
Pride Being imprisoned within your self as No. 1	Joy Feeling the exhilaration of having God as No. 1	Continuous Prayer Experiencing continuous communion with God
Greed Inflaming the passion to possess more than you have	Goodness Cultivating a character that gives rather than takes	Persistent Gratitude Experiencing the freedom of knowing that all you have comes from God

Lust Imagining how people can be used for self-interest	**Love** Practically caring for the best interests of others	**Beautiful Purity** Experiencing whole-hearted love for God and neighbor
Gluttony Looking for satisfaction through excessive consumption	**Self-Control** Being governed by godly living and the Spirit's leading	**Joyful Relinquishment** Experiencing the freedom to release a preoccupation with food and to eat more simply
Anger Using passion to manipulate and control people and circumstances	**Gentleness** Empowering others by renouncing personal agendas and expressing meekness	**Surrendered Contentment** Experiencing the satisfaction of who you are, what you have, and what you do
Sloth Doing minimal or the least important work and loving ease	**Faithfulness** Persisting in important work with utter reliability	**Life-Giving Rhythms** Experiencing a pattern of life that produces excellent work without being consumed by it
Envy Feeling pain because of someone else's advancement or possessions	**Kindness** Putting others at ease by rejoicing in their gifts and achievements	**Neighbor-Love** Experiencing the ability to meet the needs of others and to contribute to their well-being
Restlessness Thinking and feeling that there's always something better somewhere else	**Patience** Having the ability to remain where you are with meaningfulness and hope	**Vocational Confidence** Experiencing the certainty that you are in God's will and doing God's work
Boredom Having insufficient passion or interest to give yourself heartily to work and life	**Peace** Having a passion for completeness and harmony, no matter what the situation	**Heavenly-Mindedness** Experiencing the meaning and joy of work that will last in view of eternity

We hope you'll read the book from beginning to end.

You may also wish to use the matrix above as a diagnostic tool. So if you find yourself personally challenged with a specific struggle (such as "greed"), then follow the chart horizontally by reading the corresponding fruit ("goodness") and outcome ("persistent gratitude"). These interrelationships aren't set in stone, though. You'll find it helpful to review other related chapters and themes. For example, the chapter on "greed" can also be read in relation with the chapters in part 2 on "self-control," "love," and "peace," as well as the chapters in part 3 on "joyful relinquishment," "surrendered contentment," and "neighbor-love." Feel free to use the matrix, along with the thumbnail descriptions, to facilitate your reading or discussions with friends.

We hope you'll find each short chapter enriching and applicable for your life. The book can be used as a conversation-starter between spiritual friends or colleagues or among members of a small group. You could read one chapter a week for twenty-seven weeks. Or you could read the book "horizontally" — three chapters at a time (for instance, greed, goodness, and gratitude) — as the basis for a monthly group study. The exercises can be easily adapted for personal reflection or group discussion. We encourage you to seek out one or more dialogue partners, because much of spiritual growth happens in fellowship and intentional community.

The process of writing this book together has been deeply fulfilling — and salted with God's presence — as we prayed together, wrote, and edited one another's writing. We wish to thank Alvin's wife, Huey Fern, who supported us from start to finish by providing feedback and help with bibliographic research, editing, and proofreading, and doing so with wholehearted commitment and love. We are also deeply grateful to Paul's wife, Gail, for her hospitality and encouragement.

What You Can Hope to Learn by Reading This Book
- How to handle the frustrations, challenges, and ambiguities that you face every workday.
- How your work can be a source of spiritual growth rather than a hindrance.

- How your work can draw you toward God.
- How to keep God in mind while working, even if the work is all-consuming.
- How to discover God's will for you in the workplace.
- How God is most present to you in times of struggle, pain, and even failure.
- How work provides a context in which you may overcome your hidden compulsions and discover new strengths in your character.
- How your work can draw you toward God

PART ONE

Nine Soul-Sapping Struggles in the Workplace

Introducing the Deadly Work Sins

The workplace is a major arena for the battle of our souls. We spend many of our waking hours at work. We are besieged daily by hundreds of work-related thoughts and decisions that lead to good or evil. If we allow sin to burrow itself into our lives without any awareness of its toxic effects, it's as if we are handing the keys of our heart to Satan. We allow evil to mar, maul, distort, and diminish our humanity. Our relationship with God becomes strained, deceitful, or estranged.

In ways that we're not aware, there can be "sinful passions at work"(Rom. 7:5) in employee mind-sets, organizational structures, and company goals. The first step in recognizing this is to realize that sin begins in small ways — in ourselves.

Sin starts as a thought. If we mull on the thought, we will struggle between choosing good or evil. We yield to temptation when we act on an evil thought. Continuous action produces a habitual pattern that gains control of our will, our desire, our character, and our lives. When this happens, sin embeds itself deeply within us. The result is debilitating: we know that sin is destroying us but we feel helpless against its assaults. "That's who I am," we insist. "I can't change."

However, when we begin to identify and face up to the devious and diverse ways in which sin has taken root in our hearts, several things begin to happen:

- We feel grateful that God loves us even in our utter sinfulness
- We recognize that we are helpless without God
- We discover that the process of struggling against sin makes us more aware that God is with us, lovingly leading us to a fruitful outcome
- We gradually experience the freedom and joy found in Jesus Christ.

The following nine chapters seek to help us tackle the difficult questions, struggles, and issues faced in the workplace. In the Bible these are known as the "works of the flesh" that the apostle Paul outlines in Galatians 5:19-21. These inner dispositions — things such as impurity, jealousy, and anger — are ways in which sin eats us up from within. These evil impulses cause us to act as though Jesus Christ has not done his redemptive work on the cross.

Nine Soul-Sapping Struggles in the Workplace

There are all sorts of workplace sins: stealing stationery, claiming credit for work you didn't do, blaming others for your mistakes, lying, spreading gossip, calling in sick when you're not, and behaving in deceitful ways when you think nobody's watching. Such impulses are grounded in deeper soul-sapping struggles.

In the history of the church these struggles have been understood through what are called the "Seven Deadly Sins" (along with their Latin names): pride *(superbia)*, envy *(invidia)*, wrath *(ira)*, sloth *(acedia)*, avarice *(avaritia)*, gluttony *(gula)* and lust *(luxuria)*. The earliest Christian formulation of a list of deadly sins came from the desert father and theologian Evagrius of Pontus (A.D. 345-99). Evagrius and his followers went into the desert to be freed from the seductions of the world and to seek God wholeheartedly. In the desert, they found that they had to deal with themselves. In the same way, we may seek to escape from the "demons" at home by going to work, only to discover that these same "demons" have accompanied us into the workplace. Gregory the Great, the sixth-century doctor of the church who fi-

Struggles	Fruit	Outcomes
Pride	Joy	Continuous Prayer
Greed	Goodness	Persistent Gratitude
Lust	Love	Beautiful Purity
Gluttony	Self-Control	Joyful Relinquishment
Anger	Gentleness	Surrendered Content-ment
Sloth	Faithfulness	Life-Giving Rhythms
Envy	Kindness	Neighbor-Love
Restlessness	Patience	Vocational Confidence
Boredom	Peace	Heavenly-Mindedness

nalized the list of seven deadly sins we know today, observed that these sins have generative capacity: they produce offspring. "From envy there springs hatred, whispering, detraction, exultation at the misfortunes of a neighbor, and affliction at his prosperity," wrote Gregory. "From anger are produced strife, swelling of the mind, insults, clamor, indignation, blasphemies."[1]

In the same way, as we consider deadly workplace sins, we must deal with their offspring, such as overeating, eroticism, aggression, laziness and busyness, despair, restlessness, envy of other people and their gifts, and selfish ambition. No list of sins could ever be comprehensive. But we have found this traditional list of the seven deadly sins to be helpful in diagnosing our sinful predispositions. And they are deadly indeed. For example, an extreme form of sloth could result in depression, which could lead to death. Not least, the seven deadly sins continue to be prevalent and relevant in the modern workplace. To this list of seven, we've added two more — boredom and restlessness — that are especially evident at work. Boredom and restlessness are like evil twins; they sneak up to people in the workplace in ways barely recognized or acknowledged.

All nine workplace sins drain from us the will to love God and to recognize the presence of God in the workplace. These deadly sins describe the dark side of work and the worker. They explain why we often find work so frustrating, unfulfilling, sweaty, and just plain hard. However, as we cooperate with God in battling against the workplace sins (pride, greed, lust, and so on), we begin to embody what the apostle Paul calls the fruit of the Spirit of God (such as joy, goodness, and love [Gal. 5:22]). As a result, our lives become increasingly characterized by prayer, gratitude, and purity. From the matrix on page 13, you can see where we are going.

The first step toward deeper growth in God requires a deepening awareness of sin's insidious grip on our hearts and minds. We begin with pride, one of the deadliest enemies of the soul.

1

Pride: Grasping Equality with God

Struggle	Fruit	Outcome
Pride Being imprisoned within your self as No. 1	Joy Feeling the exhilaration of having God as No. 1	Continuous Prayer Experiencing continuous communion with God

AU It's good to take pride in a job well done. Or to take pride in the accomplishments of someone else. And yet we know that there's a dark side to pride. Paul, how do you see pride negatively affecting people when they work?

PS Pride makes you boast about being a self-made person. When things go well, you think you're the only one who did it. When things go bad, it's someone else's fault. You make extravagant promises. You set high expectations. But when things spiral out of control, you shift the blame elsewhere. You sincerely can't believe that all these people failed you. This happens at work all the time, Alvin.

AU I don't think people set out to be arrogant or blame-shifters. They don't make it a goal in life. And yet they turn out like that. What gives?

PS Pride blinds us from seeing the reality of who we are. It inflates our ego, distorts our vision, and walls us off from God. So we lack God's perspective. We do not seek divine help. We try to stand at the center of the universe. We trust only our-selves.

AU So if we cannot trust God, then we think we have to control everything ourselves.

PS It's easy to recognize pride in other people, but much harder to recognize these symptoms in ourselves.

AU Sounds like if we don't admit we're tempted by pride, we may already have fallen into it.

Rethinking Pride

We meet two kinds of proud people in the workplace. The first type, Mr. Solo Flyer, takes all the credit for his accomplishments. His conceit makes him chronically incapable of recognizing how he has received help along the way, especially from the people he thinks of as below him. The second type is Ms. Insufferable, who projects arrogance, treats people with disdain, and makes you feel as if the five minutes she has given you are worth more than the latest stock tip from Warren Buffett. Mr. Solo Flyer and Ms. Insuf-ferable consider themselves "superb" above all, which befits the Latin word for pride, *superbia.*

Biblical pride has a wide range of meanings. In its positive sense, pride is used to emphasize God's glory, excellence, and beauty. In contrast, when used of humanity, pride becomes dis-torted. It means attempting to appear above others, feeling con-spicuous about one's self, being haughty and puffed up by self-conceit. Pride devises schemes to toy with the weak (Ps. 10:2). Pride makes us deceive ourselves (Obad. 3). The book of Proverbs, a manual for attaining wisdom, associates pride with arrogance, evil behavior, and perverse speech.

Therefore God opposes the proud (James 4:6). In fact, he de-tests them (Prov. 16:5). Pride estranges us from God (Ps. 138:6) be-cause it encourages us to make a petty grab for equality with God, instead of attributing glory, excellence, and beauty to God. An at-titude of pride is fundamentally opposed to Jesus Christ, who did

16

not consider equality with God something to be used to his own advantage (Phil. 2:6).

Pride at Work

Pride permeates the modern workplace. Like the air we breathe, pride is absorbed into our celebrity culture, corporations, and self-image. This workplace sin often masquerades as ambition, confidence, and chutzpah. It makes us unwilling to listen to or acknowledge any painful truths about ourselves. We deceive ourselves — though not God, who sees everything. Pride is deadly because it grows so imperceptibly within us. It's killing us but we don't know it.

Bernard of Clairvaux, the remarkable eleventh-century monk, understood the anatomy of pride. As the spiritual leader of the Cistercian monastic order that influenced the commercial, intellectual, and religious life of Europe, he suggested that pride begins innocuously but gradually leads us down a precipitous ladder that results in complete estrangement from God and self.[1]

The Precipitous Ladder into Pride:
Where Are You on These Twelve Steps?

1. Being curious: Are you curious about matters that do not concern you? Curiosity seems harmless. But it's the gateway to other ills. Your curiosity about your colleague's salary could lead you to envy her, pity yourself, or strive for more.

2. Unbridled speech: Are you talking about the things you're curious about? You complain, gossip, and make passing remarks about people and affairs that don't directly impact you. You can't keep secrets.

3. Senseless optimism: Are you convincing yourself that things are always okay? The more you talk, the more you're seeking to console yourself. You focus on what you're good at. You laugh about your pain. Trivial things in life entertain you.

4. Boasting: Are you constantly hinting at or telling people about your achievements? Your compulsive need to feel good

is now expanding. You've got to tell people how great you are. You enjoy the feeling of people taking each word you say so seriously.

5. Sense of being special: Are you feeling more special than others? Your boasting makes you think you're much better than the average guy. You deserve to stand out. You're the star on your team.

6. Arrogance: Are you believing your own propaganda? You sincerely believe all the praise people are lavishing on you. You're smarter, brighter, and savvier, period.

7. Presumption: Are you thinking that you know what's best — all the time? You butt into meetings, interrupt conversations, change decisions. You don't need to ask people what they think as long as they ask you what you think.

8. Self-justification: Are you constantly explaining away your actions? If people confront you, you reply: (a) I did not do it; (b) I did it, but it was the right thing to do; (c) It was wrong, but I meant well; or (d) Someone else made me do it.

9. Insincere confession: Are you saying you're sorry only if you have to? At this point, more and more people are aware of your prideful behavior. If confronted, you're willing to shed false tears as you confess your wrongdoing. But you're not at fault, really.

10. Rebellion against peers or superiors: Are you willfully ignoring the people who are correcting, rebuking, or challenging you? You feel contempt and scorn for people and things in general. Your disdain extends to God.

11. Feeling free to sin: Are you feeling pretty good about the evil you're doing? Banish shame, fear, and guilt! Forget what moralistic people think of you. You're not governed by that. In your private moments, you may feel a tinge of regret or remorse. But you shrug it off.

12. Habitual sinning: Are you sinning with total abandonment and freedom? You can't stop even if you wanted to (but you don't). The minions of evil — lust, greed, anger, envy, and despair — control you. You have given Satan open access to the door of your heart.

Overcoming Pride

It is easy to hurtle down the many steps into pride but much harder to climb our way out of it. Given the deceitful nature of pride, efforts to extricate ourselves from the crevasse of pride could leave us in greater danger of falling deeper into it. Pride robs us of self-knowledge. For example, we know of bosses, supervisors, or associates who talk a great deal about humility and yet project arrogance in their demeanor. Such arrogance is evident to all except the proud person.

The opposite of pride is humility. Bernard of Clairvaux defines humility as "the virtue by which a man [sic] recognizes his own unworthiness because he really knows himself."[2] Such people are blessed by God with the ability to see themselves the way God sees them. They harbor no illusions about themselves and know that they cannot do anything to impress God. Yet God loves them deeply. God is delighted when such people offer themselves to God — even the broken pieces, such as failure, sorrow, and sin.

But we cannot try to achieve humility ("Friends, I've attained humility!"). Humility is a byproduct of seeking a deeper union with Jesus Christ. Jesus is the model of humility and gentleness; he will shape us into his likeness if we permit him to do so. In the same way, we cannot root out pride through direct means. We cannot work harder at self-improvement. There are, however, indirect means of dealing with pride (see the Exercises below).

Not least, the Spirit equips us with the fruit of joy, which frees us from captivity of self and gives us the exhilaration of being captivated by God and other people.

Exercises

Review the "Precipitous Ladder into Pride" and reflect on the questions. Ask God to help you determine on which step of the Ladder of Pride you are standing. Michael Casey, a Benedictine monk in Australia, has suggested some exercises that will help you cultivate humility through indirect means, depending on where you are on the ladder.[3]

1. Restrain your speech (practice this if you're anywhere between steps 1 and 3 on the Precipitous Ladder into Pride): Keeping silence doesn't come naturally in a world of noise, hurry, and crowds. Practice verbal restraint by being an intentional listener during lunch conversations this week, speaking fewer words, and asking questions motivated by genuine concern. Stop gossip or unprofitable talk.

2. Become a servant (steps 4-7): Jesus Christ demonstrated lowliness by forgetting himself and showing concern for others. Imitate Jesus as a servant in the workplace by identifying certain types of work that are usually below you (such as photocopying or washing dirty dishes left by colleagues). Do this secretly, faithfully, and with joy for one week or one month (or more).

3. Practice radical self-honesty (steps 8-12): Reflect on some sinful or habitual patterns of behavior that emerge while you work (things like irritability, perfectionism, or not tolerating mistakes). Confide in a trusted friend that you are leading a double life by continuing this behavior. Give your confidant permission to provide tough feedback, if necessary. Pray together, asking for God's help and mercy.

2

Greed: The Desire for More

Struggle	Fruit	Outcome
Greed Inflaming the passion to possess more than you have	Goodness Cultivating a character that gives rather than takes	Persistent Gratitude Experiencing the freedom of knowing that all you have comes from God

PS It's tempting to regard work purely as the means for gaining more money, more possessions, and more comforts in life. Do you struggle with that temptation, Alvin?

AU Thankfully, I don't usually think of work solely as a means for making money. In our career choices, my wife Huey Fern and I have experienced big swings in our income. We have earned far more than we needed when working in finance and investments. We have also chosen voluntary unemployment and part-time jobs. We are learning to trust God in plenty and in want. But I sometimes think, "Wouldn't it be nice to have just a little bit more?"

PS Like you and Huey Fern, my wife Gail and I have led an exciting life over the past five decades. I've counseled students, founded an inner-city church, worked as a carpenter, and taught as a professor of marketplace theology and leadership. Our income has fluctuated like crazy, sometime 50 percent down, and sometimes 100 percent up. Through all this, our lifestyle has not changed much. And now that I am retired I have no regular income.

AU So you're no longer tempted by the desire for more, right, Paul?

PS I wish. I always enjoyed using my Nikon digital SLR camera . . . until the day I had lunch with my friend Peter and saw what his newest Nikon model could do! One thing I have learned: it's not about how much money you have or earn, but about what money and possessions mean to you.

AU That sounds great. As a principle. But I'm wondering if it's possible to work in a highly paid job without becoming greedy. Or am I kidding myself?

Rethinking Greed

These days, it seems okay to be greedy, as long as you're not crass, arrogant, or grossly insensitive to other people's feelings. This outlook is spurred by organizations that reward CEOs with excessive compensation packages. Donald Trump, a real-estate mogul and television celebrity, says, "I have mixed feelings about greed being a workplace sin. I believe that you have to be motivated by some sort of insatiability for success."[1]

People usually regard greed as the drive to achieve and acquire more, in the shortest time possible. Ironically, this passion makes us feel discontented with what we have and obsessed with what we do not yet have. The fourth-century Christian monk Evagrius of Pontus, who spent the final decade of his life in prayer and scrutiny of his unruly emotions, wrote that greed is not merely the tendency to accumulate more material things. Greedy people, says Evagrius, are preoccupied with "thinking about what does not yet exist."[2] The Ten Commandments call this variant of addictive thinking "covetousness."

According to the Bible, greed or avarice (Latin: *avaritia*) is generated when our desire for God is channeled instead toward the things that God has made. At the root of greed lies the inclination to regard bread (or provision) as something distinctly separate from God. We see this dynamic at play within the heart of humanity, in the Garden of Eden, where Adam and Eve found themselves gazing at the fruit of a tree. The fruit was good for food, a delight to the eyes, and it would make them wise, they mused. In the garden of plenty, they were tempted with provision, beauty, and power. They faced an ageless conundrum that confronts us today: would they trust God to provide for their needs (in want or plenty)? Or would they satisfy those desires by whatever means seemed fit to them? Alexander Schmemann, a prominent twentieth-century Orthodox Christian priest and writer, observed that Adam's primal sin was much more than munching on a forbidden fruit: "The sin is that he ceased to be hungry for Him and for Him alone, ceased to see his whole life depending on the whole world as a sacrament of communion with God."[3]

Greed at Work

Greed is probably the most common workplace sin. It ranges from the innocuous and insidious to the garish and diabolical. Much of unrecognized greed stems from noble intentions to build a safe and secure financial base for loved ones. Even poor people are not exempt from greed.

It's easy to chuckle at the victims who fall for e-mail scams ("I am Mrs. Jewel Howard Taylor. Last year, my husband, Mr. Charles Taylor, entrusted some large quantities of diamonds to me. This is why I need you to travel to Nigeria . . ."). It's more difficult to identify how our personal spending habits, credit card purchases, and investment strategies could be motivated by greed.

It's easy to become angry with high-level executives who enrich themselves with bonuses and fat salaries while their employees are paid less than a fair wage for their work. It's also easy to rail against greedy pharmaceutical manufacturers, rapacious credit card companies, and unscrupulous banks in Third World countries. But it's much harder to identify the ways we have been co-opted by a consumer culture that makes it a norm for us to cultivate the "good life." If we're not careful, we can even use our own children as excuses to make more money for family vacations and to finance their college degrees.

The reverse side of greed is being exceedingly thrifty or stingy, hoarding things instead of being generous toward God and other people. In the parable of the talents (Matt. 25: 14-30), the servant who hoarded his one talent did so out of fear and aversion to risk. It's no fun living this way. Worse, the servant wrongly accused the master of greed, of claiming to own what did not belong to him.

One complicated way in which greed affects our thinking and actions comes in the form of advertising. Richard Pollay, professor emeritus of advertising history, notes that the advertising industry has been aggressively conducting research on how to rearrange people's thoughts and motivations about what they actually need. Modern advertising does not merely provide information to assist consumers in making rational choices among products. Through visual imagery, advertising taps into our predisposition to be discontented with what we have. "Non-wants become wants; wants become needs," says Pollay.[4]

Overcoming Greed

Greed, like all other struggles, is an indication that we were made for something more than things — we were made for God himself. We were created to be sustained by God's generosity and to depend on the provisions God has given us. In what practical ways can we overcome greed by depending on God's provision?

1. Regard shopping as a spiritual discipline: do not buy things impulsively, thoughtlessly, or simply on the siren appeal of advertising. For instance, develop a shopping list by asking ourselves what we want versus what we need.
2. Resist the siren call of pervasive advertising: be aware of how television is a doorway to thousands of "buy me" messages, and discuss with family and friends the values underlying the billboards and ads that inundate us on a daily basis.

3. Break the power of greed by giving. In a famous sermon on "The Use of Money," the Methodist preacher John Wesley once said, "Gain all you can, save all you can, give all you can."[5]

4. Expand the scope and goals of our job to include social responsibility, that is, caring for broader stakeholders and not just shareholders. (Dennis Bakke's story, related in his book *Joy at Work*,[6] is a good example of this.)

Ultimately, calling us to put to death the soul-sapping struggle of greed, God invites us to respond to the Spirit who empowers us with goodness and develops in us a character that gives rather than takes. Greed is not so much rooted out as it is expelled by the presence of something greater in the heart — the goodness of God. Such goodness, given by the Spirit, transforms us into people overflowing with gratitude. No longer inflamed by the passion to possess, we experience the freedom of knowing that all things come from God.

Exercises

1. Review the suggestions on overcoming greed (namely, shop differently, resist advertising, expand your job scope, and give generously). Brainstorm with friends or colleagues on how you can creatively apply this in your life.

2. Consider the three exhortations in Wesley's advice: "*Gain* all you can, *save* all you can, *give* all you can." In which of these areas is God calling you to grow, and what is one small step you can take? If God is calling you to grow in gaining, what steps can you take to prevent yourself from becoming greedy?

3

Lust: The Erotic Workplace

Struggle	Fruit	Outcome
Lust Imagining how people can be used for self-interest	Love Practically caring for the best interests of others	Beautiful Purity Experiencing whole-hearted love for God and neighbor

AU It just occurred to me that many offices bring together talented, attractive, and like-minded people for long hours and shared work. Mostly, we're on best behavior. But that doesn't mean that we're sexless or emotionless. How do we develop healthy relationships with people of the opposite sex without these relationships spilling into lust?

PS You are right in pointing out that the workplace can be erotic. People fall in love all the time at work. I'm sure you know of people who have gotten sexually involved with a colleague.

AU Or wish they could.

PS Not surprising, is it? After all, people work side by side for hours, days, months, and years. They dress well. They look good, and they perform at the top of their game. All this contributes to a subtle yet real eroticism in the workplace.

AU Yes, even in Asian workplaces, where people dress modestly, sexual tension can creep in. A meaningful glance. An accidental bump on the shoulder in the elevator. Lunches that last longer than usual. Office romances aside, it's not unusual to encounter dozens of sexually explicit ads on the way to work, even in a religiously conservative Islamic country.

PS Well, we cannot turn off our sexuality the moment we leave home for work, unless we play dead. It's inevitable that we come to work as whole people, including our sexual appetites.

AU Are you then implying that our sexuality could actually play a role in helping us grow spiritually when we work? Or are we playing with fire by dallying with lust and other forms of forbidden fruit?

PS I think that both could be true.

Rethinking Lust

Lust is commonly thought of as an intense sexual desire for someone else. The feelings are accompanied by a craving for gratification and excitement. From a Christian perspective, the New Testament Greek word *epithymia* is commonly translated as "lust," which is a sexual sin that perverts the God-given gift of sexuality. As with all the Seven Deadly Sins, lust begins as a thought, a disposition, or an attitude that eventually leads to action, including fornication, adultery, and other sexual perversions. Jesus said as much: "I say to you that anyone who looks at a woman with lust has already committed adultery with her in his heart" (Matt. 5:28).

Jesus' closest friend, the apostle John, identified three different ways in which lust unleashes its terrible energy.

- the cravings of sinful people, or the lust of the flesh
- the lust of their eyes
- the boasting of what they have and do (1 John 2:16 [NIV]).

Here, John alludes to how lust is interlinked with other deadly sins. Lust is similar to greed because it creates an inner craving to possess things or people that do not belong to us. Lust is also similar to pride because it generates the inward desire to boast about oneself.

The combination of greed and pride — possessiveness and inwardness — makes lust a deadly enemy. Lust is not interested in loving the other person but in treating that person as a body. It is essentially self-serving. "In lusting for the other, I really love myself," says Karl Olsson, former president of North Park Theological Seminary in Chicago. "The other becomes an instrument of my satisfaction: a bright plaything which finally grows shabby and unwanted."[1]

Sexuality in itself is good. It involves physical, psychological, and spiritual dimensions of the human person created by God. Franciscan priest Richard Rohr notes that sexuality ensures that we would never miss the fact that we are hardwired for relationship: "It is so important that we know that we are incomplete, needy and essentially social that God had to create a life-force within us that would not be silenced."[2]

Sexual arousal is normal, healthy, and good. But to allow that arousal to become a fantasy of a sexual affair with someone who is not your marriage partner means that arousal has become lust, the desire to possess another. "If your sexual desire is not guided by respect for the honor of others and regard for the holiness of God, it is lust," says theologian John Piper.[3]

This life force must therefore be directed. Protestant reformer Martin Luther famously said that it is one thing to have a bird land on your head — you can hardly stop arousing thoughts from popping up in your head from time to time. But it is quite another to let the bird build a nest there. The great saint and doctor of the church, Augustine of Hippo, wrote deeply and insightfully about the idolatrous appeal of lust in his autobiography *The Confessions.* He said lust disturbs the whole person, mingling mental and physical craving. "So intense is the pleasure that when it reaches its climax there is an almost total extinction of mental alertness; the intellectual sentries, as it were, are overwhelmed."[4]

Lust at Work

In the modern workplace, lust creeps into our hearts and minds through the Internet and office romances. Illicit use of Internet pornography in the workplace persists despite companies cracking down on inappropriate e-mails and installing blocking software. Researchers speculate that the rise of portable computers and mobile phones has made it easier to surf porn sites undetected. Meanwhile, sexual tension will continue to exist in any workplace where people with similar interests, education, and abilities find themselves unable to pursue a romantic connection for any number of reasons (including marriage, company policy enforcement, and so on). Extramarital affairs are common enough and the consequences of them are even more well-known: mutual recrimination, accusations of sexual harassment and unfair treatment, decreased work performance, and especially, emotional damage inflicted on aggrieved spouses and children. And yet four out of ten people have admitted to office flings, according to recent workplace surveys conducted in the United Kingdom and Australia.[5]

Given the pervasiveness of lust in our sexually overheated societies, it's easy to forget that lust starts with the imagination, or in the "heart," as Jesus once said (Matt. 5:28). Some forms of lust are surprisingly subtle. A friend of Paul's from New York City observed:

> Women do not sin less when it comes to our sexuality, but we do sin differently. While men lust, women cause them to lust. We know we can do this; we like it when we can do this; it is power. While men have to learn the difference between arousal and lust, attraction and obsession, lust and love, women need to learn how to attract without causing them to lust. Our job is much more difficult. While we do not assume the responsibility of men's own actions, we do often create the environment they live in.

The worst result of lust is not only the diminishment of oneself and the one lusted after, but, as every Christian who has struggled with sexual addiction knows, lust ultimately results in the loss of intimacy with God. The strange attraction of lust — for both men and women — is particularly pernicious because the sensual pleasure seems so fleeting and ephemeral compared to lust's consequences (spiritual estrangement) and love's rewards (intimacy with God). To put it bluntly: would you prioritize a sexual climax above experiencing God's love? Probably not.

Overcoming Lust

Our soul-sapping struggle with lust offers us clues to our heart's great longing for something deeper and more real: to be loved intimately by God, and to love other people with that same intimate, pure love God has for us. Love conquers lust. Lust looks to be serviced; love serves. This conversion from lust to love is a long and slow road, but we can start now, using the guiding principles and practical steps below. (It's helpful to keep in mind the admonition of Matthew the Poor, an Orthodox monk, who says that the most devoted spiritual practices cannot atone for a single sin. Rather, our unflinching focus on subduing sinful desires is simply a way of sharing our love and tender feelings toward God.)[6]

1. Know that your heart's deepest desires are for God. Hunger and passion for God put all lesser desires into perspective. Are you harboring the illicit desire to bed the spouse of another? Are you stirred by the sensuality of porn? Then consider how, in the words of Methodist Bishop William Willimon, "our God wants to make love with us, and enjoys having us, in our own fumbling ways, to make love to God."[7] Christianity is not about extinguishing desire but about directing it toward communion with the One who has created us. Such a realization will lead you into the heart of prayer.

2. Reduce exposure to erotic stimulation in your choice of movies, novels, and Internet sites. During business trips, consider the moments when you might be exposed to visual stimuli and people that could lead to sexual arousal. Put in place a plan that will help you avoid temptations (and arrange outdoor activities or visits with friends to fill the void). In a sex-saturated society, this is a life-giving spiritual discipline that helps to break lust's secret lock on your heart.

3. Pray for a colleague, a customer, or a supervisor whom you find attractive. This keeps you from treating people as bodies and gives you God's view of the person. Admitting that someone is a "delight to the eyes" becomes an opportunity to praise God for this person's beauty, since God is delightful and beautiful (see Ps. 27:4) and appreciating beauty is not in itself lust and does not necessarily lead to lust. Turning this experience into prayer can short-circuit the next unhelpful step.

4. Seek accountability partners. Prioritize time to develop trustworthy friends, or a group of peers, who care enough to ask you tough questions about your private life.

5. Identify the early beginnings of lustful thoughts. Consider the time, circumstances, and people — and any other triggers — that stir your imagination before you work, when you work, and after working hours. The more sensitive you are to lust's early beginnings, the less acute the battle will be. Your heightened vigilance also helps you become more responsive to the Spirit's gentle and quiet guidance in your heart.

Exercise

Prayerfully review the guiding principles on overcoming lust.

- Are there any specific actions that you must urgently carry out? Share your intent with a trusted friend today.
- Are there any long-term attitudes or behaviors you desire? Go for a long walk and ask God to "create a clean heart" within you (Ps. 51).

4

Gluttony: Excessive Consumption of Food

Struggle	Fruit	Outcome
Gluttony Looking for satisfaction through excessive consumption	Self-Control Being governed by godly living and the Spirit's leading	Joyful Relinquishment Experiencing the freedom to release a preoccupation with food and to eat more simply

PS I've visited food capitals around the world in the course of teaching, consulting, and coaching. Along the way, my hosts have brought me to fantastic restaurants offering sumptuous dishes. Do you think the pursuit of good food actually dulls our spiritual senses?

AU Hopefully not! Where I come from, we are serious eaters. We talk about what we're going to eat for dinner during breakfast. Business deals are clinched during a fine meal. I don't think there's anything wrong with that. But we don't reflect enough on how excessive consumption hinders us from living well. For example, with all the easy access to affordable food, I've become desensitized to the plight of an estimated one billion people in the world who do not have enough to eat.

PS Eating should revolve around communion, fellowship, and the sharing of life. When we work together, we are sharing the means of livelihood to obtain our food. Gluttony turns eating into excessive consumption. And yet, as Christians, we're usually not troubled by it. Gluttony has become a respectable sin, hasn't it?

AU It seems like we've lost the central meaning to why we eat. So, Paul, when does the appreciation of good food and good company become excessive?

Rethinking Gluttony

We usually associate gluttons with grossly obese people and ancient Roman bacchanalia. But we cannot judge gluttony by bodily appearances alone. Some obese people are "cursed" with glandular problems while other gluttonous people are "blessed" with a high metabolic rate — so that they look slim and trim even after habitual overeating. Gluttony encompasses much more than guzzling super-sized meals.

The sin of gluttony lies in finding satisfaction through excessive consumption. We use the word "gluttony" for a variety of excesses: "He is a glutton for work." "She is a glutton for punishment." "He's a glutton for attention." Gluttony is about having too much of a good thing, be it television, the Internet, sex, leisure, company, or work. Gluttony putrefies life-giving activities into addictive indulgence. Since medieval times, Christian thinkers and philosophers have linked lust and gluttony. Both indicate a lack of self-control (which, as we will see, serves as the Spirit's life-giving resource that enables us to live well).

In a narrower sense, gluttony is an inordinate preoccupation with food and eating. On a basic level, it reduces our energy for work and relationships. We become preoccupied with self-pleasure rather than caring for others. Ultimately, gluttony drives out mindfulness of God and people. The first test faced by Adam and Eve came through eating; their failure to obey resulted in alienation from God. This is tragic because God has always intended food, work, and fellowship to go together.

In the Bible, God's first gift to humankind was food (Gen. 1:29), and it is something we are taught to pray for daily (Matt.

6:11). Eating in the Bible is often a picture of God's blessing (Deut. 6:11; 8:10-12; 11:15; Ps. 23:5). It can be a means of grace (Luke 24:31; Acts 10) and a ministry (Matt. 25:35: "I was hungry," Jesus said, "and you gave me something to eat."). Eating is frequently a part of biblical festivals. In the Hebrew Bible, people were encouraged to use their tithe to buy food and drink for a festival in Jerusalem (Deut. 14:22-26). Jesus later used the feast-motif as a metaphor of God's kingdom (Luke 14:15-24), and it seems that God had in mind the wedding supper of the Lamb in the new heaven and new earth when he created the world (Rev. 19:7).

Eating includes more than mere ingestion of nourishment for survival. "The experience of taste manifests an openness to the world, tinged with wonder and appreciation," writes philosopher Leon Kass.[1] We eat to live, we eat to enjoy the fellowship of people, and we eat to experience aesthetic pleasure. On a mystical level, eating is sacramental. By faith, Christians believe in the real presence of Jesus through the bread and wine of the Eucharist (Matt. 26:17-30).

Gluttony at Work

Eating or drinking to excess is debilitating in the workplace. It results in drowsiness and reduced mental alertness. People have often acted silly, lost their dignity, or indulged in slovenly behavior as they gorged themselves on meals. Indulging in excessive food and drink — especially common in Asian business settings — could result in poor business decisions made over meals. Even business lunches on the company tab might tempt people to overindulge. More seriously, a gluttonous workforce is going to be a sick workforce. Workers will not function at maximum capacity because of the many diseases and illnesses related to obesity.

Pope Gregory I defined the vice of gluttony in five ways: "Sometimes it forestalls the hour of need; sometimes it seeks costly meats; sometimes it requires the food to be daintily cooked; sometimes it exceeds the measure of refreshment by taking too much; sometimes we sin by the very heat of an immoderate appetite."[2] This thoughtful critique has several implications, namely:

34

1. You can be a glutton by eating too often throughout the day, paying no attention to when you eat.
2. You can be a glutton by eating food that is too expensive.
3. You can be a glutton by being too fastidious about your food — consumed in large or small amounts. Some people eat as if they are gourmands and restaurant critics on the Food Network. On the opposite end of the spectrum, a gluttonous person may not crave a lot of food but insists on the "teeniest weeniest bit of really crisp toast."[3] This person is gluttonous because he or she is determined to get what he or she wants, however troublesome it may be to the host.
4. You can be a glutton by wanting more and more. Besides uncontrolled eating, one could argue that excessive preoccupation with dieting, pursued not for health but solely for beauty, is also a form of gluttony.
5. Your preoccupation with gluttony could leave you vulnerable to sin's offspring, especially lust, because both are related to the inability to control the body's excessive desires. The desert fathers and mothers were especially aware of this psycho physical link and often suggested that lust could be constrained in tandem with fasting.

Overcoming Gluttony

Godly living correlates to learning to eat in a moderate, temperate, and restrained manner. The most serious forms of gluttony are spiritual in nature: excessive consumption results in selfishness, blatant disregard for the well-being of others, indifference to suffering, living for self-gratification, and finding satisfaction in personal pleasure instead of God. Because of this, the cure for gluttony is ultimately spiritual and can be attained by following these steps:

1. Start with self-knowledge: Develop a growing awareness of your relationship with food. You may wish to record the time (or money) you spend in planning, buying, preparing, and eating food. Do you really want to consume so much time

and energy? Do you need to confess to God any excessive food compulsions? What other meaningful things would you love to do besides food-related activities?

2. Lifestyle changes: Take small steps in reforming your lifestyle and attitudes related to food. For example, you could practice a modest form of partial fasting by deciding not to eat desserts except on special occasions.

3. Thanksgiving: Learn to give thanks for available food rather than always craving something else or something more. "The right food," writes Clement of Alexandria, "is thanksgiving."[4] The food we eat is a constant reminder that we depend on God's faithfulness and goodness. Paul says the same thing: "So, whether you eat or drink, or whatever you do, do everything for the glory of God" (1 Cor. 10:31).

Ultimately, Jesus says that our perspective toward food and work reveals whether we trust God — or worry excessively about daily provision: "Steep your life in God-reality, God-initiative, God-provisions. Don't worry about missing out. You'll find all your everyday human concerns will be met. Give your entire attention to what God is doing right now, and don't get worked up about what may or may not happen tomorrow" (Matt. 6:33-34, *The Message*).

Exercise

Gluttony is not just about eating too much but also includes your attitude toward food. Answer these questions to determine both your behavior and your attitude:

- Is your concentration at work affected because you're thinking about food?
- Do you snack too much before and after meal times?
- Do you spend too much money on food and drink?
- Do you obsess about the quality of food? Are you annoyed, or do you complain excessively, when a dish fails to meet your expectations?

- Are you a picky eater?
- Do you eat or drink too much, and do you do it too eagerly?

Prayerfully reflect on Matthew 6:33-34 *(The Message)* and look out for opportunities this coming week to apply these verses in your life.

5

Anger: The Burning Desire to Control

Struggle	Fruit	Outcome
Anger Using passion to manipulate and control people and circumstances	Gentleness Empowering others by renouncing personal agendas and expressing meekness	Surrendered Contentment Experiencing the satisfaction of who you are, what you have, and what you do

AU Most of us don't think of ourselves as walking time bombs. We don't usually get mad at coworkers, scheme against bosses, or punch our fists against the wall. We don't humiliate others or stoke people into a rage. We try to be nice. And yet, do you think that deep down, we all struggle with anger in some way or other?

PS Typically we think of an angry person as the tough and mean cigar-chomping Big Boss who thinks it's okay to goad, bully, intimidate, or shout as long as he gets the job done. But what about when we seethe in silence when our colleague steals our idea and gets all the credit? Isn't that anger, too?

AU Or when we stare contemptuously at people who show up late for meetings?

PS Or get frustrated with the spouse who tells us we're working too hard?

AU Or when we marinate in self-disgust after flubbing our presentation in front of the chairperson of the board?

PS Or sometimes we just feel a nagging irritability throughout the day. And we get madder at ourselves for not being able to pinpoint the cause.

AU Some nights, as I get ready for bed, I see the face of the offender in my mind's eye. And I'm playing and replaying that awful scene, earlier in the day, when he or she yelled at me for something that wasn't my fault. Boy, I feel like yelling right back.

PS It's so easy to get angry when things spiral out of control.

AU Yeah, I'm getting angry about all the ways that I can't control anger!

Rethinking Anger

"On a business terrain, the player who fights without anger is at a distinct disadvantage, because the real guns out there are furious all the time, and are truly happy only if they are stomping on the face that they have just torn from the bleeding skull of their despised adversary," wrote Stanley Bing in his book, *Sun Tzu Was a Sissy: Conquer Your Enemies, Promote Your Friends, and Wage the Real Art of War.* "Other than patience and a hollow leg, anger is the single most important personal attribute that a warrior can possess."[1]

Bing, the irreverent columnist for *Fortune* magazine, wrote tongue-in-cheek, but he's probably correct in surmising that most people use anger as a powerful tool to manipulate and control other people and circumstances.

Anger, one of the classic Seven Deadly Sins, shows up in countless ways where we live and work: general harassment, whether sexual or some other form; favoritism of one employee over another; criticisms of employees in front of staff or clients, or behind their backs; withdrawal of earned benefits; betrayal of trust and poor communication.

Anger becomes sin when it is allowed to boil over without restraint, resulting in a "sawed-off shotgun" reaction that hurts everyone in earshot and leaves devastation in its wake, often with irreparable consequences. "A fool gives full vent to anger," says the writer of Proverbs (29:11). Rather than speaking the truth in love, we allow rotten and destructive words to pour from our lips (Eph. 4:15, 29). Anger also becomes sin when one clams up, doing the "slow burn." This causes one to become irritable and fly off the handle over any little thing, often things unrelated to the underlying problem.

But not all anger is destructive. In the Bible, anger is described as a burning, seething force that can be aroused in human beings and also in God. Two Greek words are used in the New Testament for our English word "anger." One *(orgē)* means "passion, energy"; the other *(thymos)* means "agitated, boiling." Biblically, anger is God-given energy intended to help us solve problems. Biblical examples of constructive uses of anger include Paul confronting Peter because of his wrong example (Gal. 2:11-14), David being upset over hearing Nathan the prophet sharing an injustice (2 Sam. 12), and Jesus getting angry over how some Jews had defiled the Gentiles' place of worship at God's temple in Jerusalem (John 2:13-18).

Paul implies that not all anger is sin when he writes, "In your anger do not sin" (Eph. 4:26). The spiritual fathers of the church observe that anger has great force to fight against demons or destroy evil thoughts. "Expressing anger can be God-pleasing and constructive when our underlying motivation is to restore relationships, fight injustice, or battle evil," writes Tomas Spidlik, a scholar from the Eastern Orthodox tradition.[2]

Though present in God in the form of righteous anger, and harnessed by Jesus Christ as zeal for God's house, most forms of anger residing within us are destructive. Anger turns to sin when it is selfishly motivated (James 1:20), or when it is allowed to linger (Eph. 4:26-27). Instead of using the energy generated by anger to attack the problem at hand, one attacks the person instead.

Anger at Work

Of all our emotions, anger is the most explosive, often raw-edged, and a catalyst for other destructive forces such as envy, pride, depression, and even murder. Even when we try to suppress anger, we do violence to our inner selves and can irreparably hurt our loved ones. Anger freezes over a warm and generous heart, leaving behind a permafrost of politeness and niceness (punctuated by icicles of resentment and sarcasm). If left unchecked, this could lead to depression. The thoughts of wounding others results in wounding oneself. Anger will make us sabotage friendships, professional relationships, and community life. Ultimately we become estranged from God, because angry people find they cannot pray.

John Cassian, a fourth-century theologian, has reflected extensively on how anger can potentially rupture community life, especially within the two monasteries he founded in Europe. His insights are especially relevant to the modern workplace (and the church, too), where anger is disguised or suppressed by forced smiles and cordial e-mails.

1. He warns against short-term solutions in dealing with anger. We could try to conceal our annoyance or pretend to smooth things over or seek false peace. But Cassian suggests that is a Band-Aid solution. Our cool demeanor creates a more terrible problem: we become scornful of others.[3]

2. We face double jeopardy when we use silence and derision as weapons to provoke others into anger: "A spiteful silence surpasses the harshest verbal abuse, and the wounds of enemies are more easily borne than the sly compliments of mockers."[4]

3. The poisonous effects of anger become deeply embedded when we seek to be nice to one another even though deep down, we harbor hatred. Cassian warns against toxic relationships in which we attempt to preserve a veneer of niceness. Too easily, we become like Judas who offered a "feigned greeting and a kiss of deceitful love."[5]

4. Often we're unable to tell that we're suppressing anger. But our bodies don't lie, suggests Cassian. Suppressed anger often leads to loss of appetite, sleeplessness, and fantasies of controlling people.[6] At the heart of anger is the desire to control.

41

Overcoming Anger

Companies have attempted to contain the radioactive results of workplace anger through anger management seminars, executive coaching to help CEOs overcome fits of rage, and even yoga and meditation classes. Other strategies include conflict resolution, taking a time-out, positive self-talk, managing stress, and developing EQ (emotional intelligence) skills.

Cassian, who spent decades observing how disputes were mediated among monks, suggests four ideas for dealing with anger that are applicable in the workplace: ensure you remain calm in your lips as well as the depths of the heart; do not speak in rage; say no to vengeance; and ask God to enlarge your heart so that the turbulent waves of wrath will be dissipated in the harbor of love.[7] These restraints on the mouth and the heart are crucial when people work in teams.

Generally, we should not try to eradicate anger head-on, lest we become even more angry when we fail or realize we cannot control anger. Rather, overcoming anger requires indirect means of surrendering to God the desire to control. This includes:

1. Cultivating meekness: the first step is to confess your struggles with anger before God. Do not fret over your own imperfections. Of course, you must rightly be displeased and sorry when you commit wrongs, but it is usually a sign of your desire to control when you become angry at being angry. Meek people are not shocked by sin; they admit their struggles to God and to others.

2. Cutting off anger at the roots: become aware of the early beginnings of anger in your heart and how it grows from a tiny seed into a redwood tree. Should you find yourself becoming angry, do not suppress anger in a violent or forceful manner, which will only exacerbate the situation. Rather, cry out to God for mercy.

3. Fostering gentleness when you aren't angry: if you are naturally loud, speak gently to colleagues and loved ones. Pray for your enemies. Forgive others as Jesus forgave. When you

practice this, you will discover that you are deeply loved by God, who has restrained godly anger against you and embraced you as a child.

Anger, purified by love and gentleness, can become a powerful force of transformation in the workplace. We will no longer use anger to manipulate and control people and circumstances. Rather, with the Spirit's help, we will naturally renounce personal agendas and seek to build people up.

Exercises

1. Identify five instances of frustration in your workplace. Review the ways in which you might have suppressed or disguised anger in each of these moments:
   - Did you conceal your annoyance?
   - Did you seek false peace?
   - Did you use silence as a form of retaliation?
   - Did you pretend to be nice to people you despise?
   - Did you suffer from insomnia and loss of appetite because of workplace stress?
2. In your desire to become a more gentle soul, prayerfully consider how you can creatively apply Cassian's four suggestions on overcoming anger.

6

Sloth: Pathological Busyness

Struggle	Fruit	Outcome
Sloth Doing minimal or the least important work and loving ease	Faithfulness Persisting in important work with utter reliability	Life-Giving Rhythms Experiencing a pattern of life that produces excellent work without being consumed by it

AU Paul, how do you find the time to attend to the important things when there are so many competing, urgent demands?

PS What's going on in your life that prompts you to ask this question?

AU The past few weeks have been really crazy. There's just too much going on: multiple deadlines, new projects, an overseas trip. But I'm pretty sure the crazy stuff will blow over in a few months' time. Then I will get serious about spending more time with my wife during the weekends. And stop checking the Blackberry after midnight.

PS You sound pathologically busy.

AU At least I'm not lazy. I'm not idle. I don't neglect my duties. I don't laze around with a piña colada five days a week. Better to be busy than lazy.

PS My hunch is that the workaholic and the lazy bum are closer to one another than you think.

Rethinking Sloth

Some people seem to harbor a severe aversion to work. Their habits remind us of the three-toed sloth in the Amazon that hangs upside down from branches and moves so sluggishly that moss grows on its sun-drenched belly. Similarly, slothful people slouch along in stupefied apathy, allowing their talents to wither away. At work, their lazy habits become reprehensible, as they work diligently to avoid work, resulting in more work for their colleagues.

"There are few things I hate more than laziness," said real estate mogul and TV celebrity Donald Trump. "I work very, very hard and I expect the people who work for me to do the same. If you want to succeed, you cannot relax. . . . I never take vacations because I can't handle the time away from my work. I recently read that these days, a high percentage of the people who do take vacations tend to check e-mail and voice mail and call in to the office when they leave. Those are the people I want working for me."[1]

Trump misses the point here. Lazy people aren't the only ones who are slothful. Extremely busy people can also be slothful. Consider the symptoms of workaholics: they ignore family and loved ones; they ignore pain signals telegraphed by their bodies; and they are self-absorbed. They treat people in a perfunctory manner. And without the high-adrenaline buzz of work, they feel useless, listless, guilty, and depressed. Such withdrawal symptoms are strangely similar to someone who's chronically lazy.

The book of Proverbs inveighs against the sluggard and praises hard work. But there are more nuances to the matter than what appears at first sight. Derek Kidner, in his commentary on Proverbs, observes that the slothful will not begin things, will not finish things, and will not face up to things. Here, it is assumed that even the slothful person works. The heart of the problem lies in the fact that the morally and spiritually lazy person is someone who prefers to whittle away at lesser problems while refusing to attend to the most important work at hand. "Consequently, he is restless with unsatisfied desire," says Kidner, and "helpless in the face of the tangle of his affairs."[2] The slothful person's appetite is never filled

(Prov. 13:4). To be more exact, the slothful individual actually has a huge desire to do what is righteous but simply refuses to spring into action to do what must be done (Prov. 21:25-26).

The chronically lazy person chooses to do minimal work while the work-obsessed person exerts tremendous energy doing less important work. In both cases, they harm themselves and the people around them. Sloth has also deadened their spiritual senses from being attuned to the work of God.

Sloth at Work

When we consider how sloth creeps its way into the workplace, five kinds of slothful personalities come to mind:

1. Indulgent Irene drifts from one amusement to another. She despises the daily tedium of work. She thinks of life as an endless cruise on the Aegean sea: no stress, no tears, no anxiety, no decisions except what to eat and where to sun oneself. Unfortunately, such a dream world doesn't exist.
2. Holy Harry works sluggishly during the day but perks to life the moment he leaves the office and walks into church. He refuses to invest himself fully in the workplace, claiming that his day job is "secular" and pays the bills but has no bearing on serving God. Despite Harry's zeal, he undermines his Christian witness due to his half-hearted attitude at work.
3. Disengaged Diana has tuned herself out. She works for a salary but does not want to make a difference. Though present in body, her mind is elsewhere. She is uninvolved, uncommitted, uncaring. Diana may not think that she's a problem, but her attitude demoralizes her coworkers and sucks energy out of the room.
4. Abdicating Andrew likes being a spectator. He ignores the needs of the world around him, including people in dire trouble. He looks the other way when he thinks someone's asking for help. Do not count on him to speak up for truth, especially when that requires any personal sacrifice.

5. Extreme Evelyn is the most common manifestation of a modern-day sluggard. She's a highly talented knowledge worker who loves her job and feels validated by her accomplishments. Evelyn has been bequeathed the perks of an ultimate road warrior, including a Blackberry, business class travel, and a bottomless expense account. Her work is often alluring, exciting — and accompanied by the adrenaline rush of clinching deals or completing projects.

In a December 2006 article published in the *Harvard Business Review,* Sylvia Ann Hewlett and Carolyn Buck Luce studied people who held "extreme jobs," that is, highly paid professionals who work sixty hours or more per week and hold jobs with at least five of the following characteristics:

- Unpredictable flow of work
- Fast-paced work under tight deadlines
- Inordinate scope of responsibility that amounts to more than one job
- Work-related events outside regular work hours
- Availability to clients 24/7
- Responsibility for profit and loss
- Responsibility for mentoring and recruiting
- Large amount of travel
- Large number of direct reports
- Physical presence at the workplace at least ten hours a day.[3]

The financial payoff for such hard work can be huge. There are, however, numerous hidden costs. Most extreme workers say they don't get enough sleep or exercise; they overeat; they neglect relationships with children; and after a twelve-hour day, they feel too tired to even talk to their spouses. They don't properly maintain their homes. They are unwilling to do manual labor — from putting out the trash to scrubbing the toilet.

Workaholism brings spiritual dangers as well. Since it causes people's brains to shut down, they have no energy to think about anything other than work — not about relationships, marriage, children, health, parents, church, relationship with God, and especially matters of eternal consequence. They are waiting for life to get less busy; then they'll put things right. But chances are, they will doggedly persist in doing the same things over and over again. They will toil in jobs that violate their basic principles, even when survival does not absolutely demand it. They work obsessively until they lose the capacity for self-awareness. With their inner vigilance lulled to sleep by sloth, they linger on in settings that steadily kill their spirits.

"Slothful people," says Frederick Buechner, "may be very busy people. They are people who . . . fly on automatic pilot. Like somebody with a bad head cold, they have mostly lost their sense of taste and smell. They know something's wrong with them, but not wrong enough to do anything about it."[4]

Overcoming Sloth

Jesus Christ offers us a sharply contrasting model that has huge implications for how we work. When accused of healing a man with paralysis on the Sabbath, Jesus said: "My Father is still working, and I also am working" (John 5:17). Jesus did not abdicate when he saw desperate need; nor did he use Sabbath laws to justify inaction. In contrast to the sluggard, Jesus was fully responsive to the Father. He sprang into action and healed the man.

Yet Jesus was no workaholic. He realized his limitations and harbored no illusions about self-sufficiency. He put it starkly: "Very truly, I tell you, the Son can do nothing on his own" (John 5:19). A person like Jesus with a profound self-knowledge and God-knowledge would never fall into the trap of work addiction. The key to effective and godly action lies in seeing God's action in our world. Such inner sight requires discernment that enables us to become like ants that innately know the best season for harvesting food (Prov. 6:6-11).

We are hewing at the roots of sloth when we resolve to be faithful to both great and small tasks. "Great opportunities to serve God rarely present themselves but little ones are frequent,"

48

says Francis de Sales, who wrote *Introduction to the Devout Life,* a classic guide on the spiritual life.[5] We break the choke hold sloth has on us when we learn to be at peace with housework, calmly washing dishes and "doing the meanest household chores cheerfully and filled with love and affection for God."[6] The preacher arranges chairs; the CEO throws away trash in the office; the manager waters a colleague's geraniums. All around us, in the workplace and our neighborhoods, there are always humble duties we can do for God's pleasure. Mother Teresa was a great example of this. "In this life we cannot do great things. We can only do small things with great love," she says in that gravelly voice of hers in "Mother Teresa: The Legacy," the deeply moving documentary film directed by Ann and Jeanette Petrie.

Finally, the practice of Sabbath — resting from work for a twenty-four-hour day — can be part of the process of overcoming sloth. People on a treadmill of working harder and harder to support a particular lifestyle desperately need this.[7] Sabbath is not merely cessation from work. A sabbatical life grants us God's big view of the meaning of our lives as we entrust our work to the God who "neither slumbers nor sleeps" (Ps. 121).

Exercise

Review the five personalities listed above (from Indulgent Irene to Extreme Evelyn). Do you embody any of their attributes? If so, prayerfully ask God to change your attitude towards work. Share your hopes and any specific next steps with a friend.

7

Envy: The Pain of Another's Advancement

Struggle	Fruit	Outcome
Envy Feeling pain because of someone else's advancement and possessions	Kindness Putting others at ease by rejoicing in their gifts and achievements	Neighbor–Love Experiencing the ability to meet the needs of others and to contribute to their well-being

AU I feel sheepish for admitting this. But why is it that I feel displeasure when somebody else is succeeding?

PS Any specific example come to mind?

AU It seems so trivial. During a planning meeting, a colleague got up and started to sketch a chart on the white board — a really elaborate one, with boxes within boxes, bullet points, and arrows pointing this way and that. He incorporated everyone's feedback. The strategy, the goals, the next steps, and the detailed action plan were all there. He drew it perfectly the first time. Most importantly, it galvanized the team and spurred everyone to action. I should have been rejoicing with my colleague. But instead, I asked myself, "Why couldn't I have done that?" I felt sorry that I didn't have his skills and experience.

PS No one is exempt from struggling with envy, especially in the workplace, where we are so prone to comparing our achievements with those of others. Frederick Buechner, a pastor and prize-winning author, says that "Envy is the consuming desire to have everybody else as unsuccessful as you are."[1]

AU I can see how envy transforms me into a "negatron." Rather than valuing my gifts and celebrating the gifts of other people, I berate myself and disparage their accomplishments. It's awful.

PS At least you're able to recognize the early signs of envy. Some of us are eaten up by envy and we don't even know it.

Rethinking Envy

Envy is a primal sin among the Seven Deadly Sins. The ancient doctors of the soul considered envy, along with pride, the most intractable and pernicious of the seven deadlies, more so than lust or anger. Envy fuses together jealousy and selfish ambition. It is described as demonic (James 3:16). It is a magnet for other vices. It compounds the effects of other deadly sins. Envy is diabolical, said Saint Augustine of Hippo, because we rejoice when we see the misfortune of a neighbor and feel displeasure when we see someone prosper.[2]

Not surprisingly, many theologians and spiritual directors consider envy or jealousy a deadlier foe than anger. "Wrath is cruel, anger is overwhelming, but who is able to stand before jealousy?" observes the writer of Proverbs (27:4). Like cancer, envy consumes our inner being. It "makes the bones rot" (Prov. 14:30).

In the Hebrew Scriptures, envy is usually related to jealousy, rivalry, and misplaced zeal. We are shown that envy distorts good intentions by imbuing them with evil; the end result is usually terrible. Cain longs for God's approval but he falls into envy and kills his favored brother. Rachel yearns to bear a child but envy causes her to detest her sister's fertile womb. Saul, who aches for his people's approval, drives himself mad (literally) with envy as he mobilizes his troops to hunt down David, his protégé. The prime example of how envy putrefies good intentions into greater evil can be found in the behavior of the chief priests who delivered Jesus to his death. These religious leaders convinced themselves that they were acting for the good of their nation, but the Gospel writers, who reflect God's perspective, pointed out that the chief priests did it "out of envy" (Matt. 27:18 [TNIV]).

Paradoxically, the more we grow in virtue, the more susceptible we are to envy. So even after Peter was forgiven and commissioned three times by Jesus to feed his sheep (John 21), Peter couldn't help being curious about whether the Lord was treating a fellow disciple more favorably. "What about John?" Peter quizzed Jesus. But Jesus replied simply that it was none of Peter's business.

Envy at Work

Envy often begins when we compare ourselves to those around or above us. We hear voices in our head saying, "I deserve this more than that lazy, good-for-nothing fellow sitting next to me." "Why did she get promoted when I got passed over?" "Why am I being treated so unfairly compared to so-and-so?"

Inevitably, such comparisons cause us to resent our station in life and envy someone else's calling. A homemaker might resent her seemingly invisible status and envy her spouse, whose office work gains him public praise. We might demean our tasks at hand, while casting an envious eye on someone else's project that appears to be fast-tracked for success. It doesn't help that most companies today function in a global environment where winning is prized: it's okay to tear down the reputations of the organizations and rivals we envy.

Envy can be legitimized by company policies, societal norms, and national legislation, causing greater conflict between the haves and have-nots. Those who enjoy the entitlements (be they senior management, political leaders, or certain socioeconomic groups) often cling to their rights and privileges, even when it's clear that others will suffer. Meanwhile, the have-nots who stew in resentment are waiting for the day when the privileged will be punished. In both cases, envy causes people to drag other people down. Dorothy Sayers, the twentieth-century literary critic and author, calls envy "the great leveler": if it cannot level things up, it will level them down. "Rather than have anyone happier than itself, it will see us miserable together," says Sayers.[3]

Among Christians, envy can take the form of spiritual competitiveness. It is easy to envy those who appear to preach better, teach better, or even pray better. Envy is sinister because its early beginnings are so mixed up with good things. In fact, our desire for greater good could be the very thing that arouses our envy: a winsome personality; effectiveness in Christian ministry; polished education; vivacious children; a seemingly trouble-free existence. We might even long for "holy" things: a seat on the church committee; theological education; or recognition by others as a wise leader.

Hardly anyone admits to suffering from full-blown envy. We naturally learn to disguise its ugliness, and this makes it difficult to recognize the evil of envy — even its minor forms — in ourselves.

As with all the other workplace struggles, envy follows a progression: It begins in the mind, seeps into our feelings, slips onto our tongue, and gets played out in action.

- Looking: Envy begins with looking around. For example, you measure yourself against people who are similar to you. How much money are they making? What are they driving, wearing, seeing, and doing? You feel anxious and resentful. At this stage you're not sinning. You're simply looking.
- Self-pity: The more you look, the more you feel sorry for yourself. You're disgusted by his success. You're dejected because you deserve the glory, not him. At this stage, envy has penetrated your thoughts.
- Guerrilla warfare: You verbalize your thoughts, anxiety, and resentment. You gossip, spread rumors, and find small, indirect ways to tear down her accomplishments through backhanded compliments and faint praise. You're actively sinning through your words of envy.
- Full-blown war: Your words become action. Day and night, you plot how to actively destroy his reputation — or deprive him of happiness. You even enlist conspirators to spite him,

directly and indirectly. You're now in envy's thrall. And you're probably the most miserable person in your office right now.

Overcoming Envy

Envy has no easy remedies. You must be ever vigilant against this chameleon-like foe. We suggest the following steps:

- Guard your eyes. What things do you see that cause you to compare yourself with other people?
- Stop feeling sorry for yourself. Become aware of "poor me" words and thoughts.
- Don't spread even the slightest rumor about your neighbor or do anything that assassinates your colleague's character.
- Kill envy by teaching yourself to be grateful for whatever God has given you, whether big or small, whether water or dryness.

The exact opposite of envy's grasping nature is found in Jesus' call for us to love our neighbors as ourselves. Envy is the only one of the Seven Deadly Sins that is listed in the Ten Commandments: "You shall not covet . . . anything that belongs to your neighbor" (Exod. 20:17). This commandment, taken positively, challenges us with two questions. First, do we love God enough to be content with whatever we are given? And second, do we love our neighbor enough to not covet what she has?

In loving our neighbor, we embody kindness — a fruit that results from life in the Holy Spirit. We rejoice over our colleagues' gifts and achievements, as if these were our own (James 2:8). Rather than tearing people down with our words and actions, we become natural at putting people at ease.

Exercises

1. Recall one recent event at your workplace where you found yourself feeling envious. Where were you on the progression

of envy (looking, self-pity, guerrilla warfare, or full-blown war)? Write a prayer of confession and ask God for healing.

2. On a daily basis, identify five to ten things that give you joy. Give thanks to God for them.

8

Restlessness: The Desire to Run Away

Struggle	Fruit	Outcome
Restlessness Thinking and feeling that there's always something better somewhere else	Patience Having the ability to remain where you are with meaningfulness and hope	Vocational Confidence Experiencing the certainty that you are in God's will and doing God's work

PS You've worked in six jobs, in six different fields, and in four different countries, Alvin. And you're still in your thirties. Have you ever struggled with restlessness or the thought that there's always something better out there?

AU For sure. We live in a business culture where people are rewarded for notching up skills and competencies by moving around to different companies or divisions within the shortest possible time. By positioning myself as a relentless learner who thrives on acquiring new skills, I am rewarded for restlessness!

PS You sound rather pleased with yourself. Too pleased, in fact.

AU You might be right. Do you think restlessness is a spiritual ailment?

PS It can be. One consequence of restlessness is that if you're constantly moving, or constantly running away from problems, you will not face up to your true self. Old problems will resurface. If you had trouble delivering on promises in your old company, you'll probably over-promise and under-deliver in the new company. People who move around too much often lose the capacity for thoughtful reflection.

AU Ouch. Maybe I should reflect more thoughtfully on this issue.

Rethinking Restlessness

Certain kinds of jobs are inclined to cause restlessness: the deskbound writer churning out lifeless ad copy; the preparation cook cubing carrots for the stockpot; the high-school teacher grading badly written essays; the accountant wading through Excel spreadsheets. Most jobs that involve continuous stress, repetition, or solitary work will drive us to distraction or induce in us the urge to run away and do something else. However, people who are engaged in highly stimulating work can also feel the itch of restlessness. Many people feel they are laboring in the wrong career, while others find success but no satisfaction in their jobs. They can't shrug off the thought that there's always something better out there.

Evagrius of Pontus, the fourth-century theologian who possessed a brilliant, intuitive understanding of the inner life, classified these thoughts and feelings as *acedia,* a term that has no equivalent in modern language. *Acedia* is marked by a profound restlessness that leaves us agitated, discouraged, and ungrateful for our present circumstances. In our jet-setting culture of mobility, job-hopping, and globalization, restlessness might seem integral to life. To be called a "road warrior" or "global nomad" often confers prestige and respect. Not so for Evagrius. Among a pantheon of sins, Evagrius classified *acedia* as one of the eight deadly thoughts[1] that lead us away from allegiance to Jesus Christ.

Acedia has been called the "noonday demon" because it usually attains its greatest force during the day. At the most basic level, *acedia* is deadly because it causes us to despise our present circumstances, our work, and even life itself. At the same time, this spiritual sickness drives us to desire things that are tantalizingly out of reach. We run madly from place to place, searching for something or someone to bring satisfaction to longings we do not know how to describe. "*Acedia* wages a two-pronged attack, an entangled struggle of hate and desire," writes monastic scholar William Harmless.[2] The prophet Isaiah likened restless people to the troubled sea whose constant movement churns up muck and mire (Isa. 57:20-21).

Not all forms of restlessness are harmful, though. Jacob, from the Hebrew Scriptures, and the woman from Samaria, from the Christian Scriptures, embodied such restlessness. Jacob wandered from place to place seeking one blessing after another but never finding what he truly wanted. In the same way, the unnamed Samaritan woman lingered in the noonday sun, thirsting after something deeper. Their restlessness ultimately drove them into the arms of God. The brilliant theologian, Saint Augustine of Hippo, who struggled with restlessness throughout his twenties and thirties, observed in his *Confessions:* "You have made us for yourself, O Lord, and our hearts are restless until they rest in you."[3]

Restlessness at Work

The first sign of restlessness at work occurs when we carry out our tasks half-heartedly — though we might be present in body, we are absent in spirit. Gradually we begin to abdicate our responsibilities, justifying this by saying they are really other people's work. We learn the art of office tai chi, using our hands and feet to ward off assignments headed our way and diverting work to other people's desks. Perversely, even as we become lackadaisical workers, we fantasize about how we could be doing great things for God in some faraway place, like helping missionaries haul medical supplies into the hilly regions of Sulawesi for suffering villagers.

Acedia afflicts workplace people in subtle ways. Do we perpetually think of changing jobs, advancing our careers, or waiting for that special call from the headhunter? Sometimes this masks a deeper problem. For example, after we have switched jobs for the fourth time in three years, it's no surprise if we find the same issues boomeranging back — with even greater force — in our new place of work. Unresolved relationships and misunderstandings have a tendency to do that. If this is your track record, running away does not help. It only makes things worse.

Benedict of Nursia, a sixth-century expert on community life, warned his monks about adopting the lifestyle of a "sarabite" (person who lives without principles) or a "gyrovague" (person whose law is to do whatever strikes the fancy). Such people are always on the move, never settling down. They are not rooted in community. Such constant movement and rootlessness will result in a downfall, warns Benedict.[4]

In our approach toward work, do we behave like sarabites or gyrovagues? Are we guided by a rule of life? Or do we simply go where we like and do what we like?

Overcoming Restlessness

The first step in struggling against the spirit of restlessness is choosing not to run away. To remain rooted where we are (even if for a season) requires us to be committed to our work, family, community, and country, in good times and bad. We must see that God wants to teach us lessons in the present moment. A short story in the fourth-century literature of the desert fathers depicts a young man traveling a great distance to seek out a famous monk for spiritual advice. The old man discerned that the younger fellow was trying to run away from his "cell" — the learning space to which he was called to work and pray. So the old man advised the younger one: "Stay in your cell, and your cell will teach you everything."[5]

If you choose to remain where you are, here is what you might discover:

1. You see reality as it is. You cease to live in a fantasy world daydreaming about what-ifs. Instead of casting around for short-term fixes (like that lucrative job in Dubai), you realize that

you must first change yourself. Or, to be more precise, you are now ready for God to change you. You realize you are stuck with these people: your family, your colleagues, your neighbors, your compatriots. And you had better make the best of the situation. So you begin to listen. You become more attentive to people, events, and issues that you used to ignore. (Part of seeing things as they are could mean acknowledging that there are situations — such as a toxic workplace or being stuck in an abusive situation — which entail the need to move on rather than remain.)

2. You discover that your present situation is exactly the soil needed for nurturing the virtuous life. There is no point for a married man to dream of the prolonged solitude of the monk. The middle-manager should not pine for the simple life of a student or the relaxing life of a retired CEO. "These useless desires usurp the place of virtues I ought to have — patience, resignation, mortification, obedience, and meekness under suffering. They are what God wishes me to practice at this time," says the seventeenth-century spiritual director Francis de Sales.[6]

3. You gain the wisdom of knowing when to move on without running away. You become more perceptive to God calling you — like Abraham — to trust and follow God further down the path of downward mobility, relinquishment, and self-surrender. Sometimes this call comes unexpectedly, just as you think you'll remain where you are for the rest of your life. Quite evidently, such a call will not come while you are struggling with the urge to run away.

4. You celebrate and use what gifts and talents you actually have, not what you wish you possessed. The flipside is also true: you stop fantasizing about acquiring more and better talents to serve God, and begin the patient process of honing the skills and abilities that God has already given you.

The masters of the spiritual life through all ages say that when we choose not to run away — in person or in spirit — we will ultimately grow in love. We learn commitment and fidelity. We are no longer controlled by the demonic impulse to rush headlong into greener pastures. We discover more of God's faithfulness. We find security in God. We are content with who we are, what we have, and where we are. We are where God wants us to be. And we are free.

Exercise

Draw a time-line of your life by listing the date for every major career move or job change you've experienced up to today.

- At any point, was your job change motivated by the desire to run away?
- Identify the names of the people who influenced you and impacted how you worked at each stage.
- What did you learn in each situation?
- Thank God for the growth you experienced in dealing with any struggles or difficult situations.

9

Boredom: Slow Death in the Workplace

Struggle	Fruit	Outcome
Boredom Having insufficient passion or interest to give yourself heartily to work and life	Peace Having a passion for completeness and harmony, no matter what the situation	Heavenly-Mindedness Experiencing the meaning and joy of work that will last in view of eternity

AU Is boredom a serious spiritual issue for Christians in the marketplace? I'd think that most of us are over-stimulated rather than bored. Have you ever been plagued by boredom while you worked?

PS For a whole year I was bored to death with my work as a religious bureaucrat. Lots of repetitious, mindless work. It was numbing. My wife had to give me a book to read on the adventure of living! Have you ever been bored at work, Alvin?

AU I have always worked for companies that seek to be fast-paced, innovative, and creative. They reward "engaged employees" who love their jobs and are willing to go the extra

---

This chapter is adapted from R. Paul Stevens, "Boredom," in Robert Banks and R. Paul Stevens, eds., *The Complete Book of Everyday Christianity* (Downers Grove, Ill.: InterVarsity Press, 1997), pp. 80-83.

mile for their companies. So my gut response is to say, no, I'm not bored. And yet . . .

PS And yet what?

AU It's possible for an all-consuming job to generate a reverse kind of boredom. If the pace is always intense, if there's constant change and perpetual motion, if we're always stimulated, it's possible to go into sensory overload. As a foreign correspondent, I spent several years writing about crises, conflicts, and calamities in the region. It was stimulating at first. But after some time, a kind of ennui set in. "There's nothing new under the sun," my colleagues and I would sigh, as we jetted off to cover yet another political-sex-corruption-environmental-(you-fill-in-the-blank) scandal.

PS When we're bored, it feels like "slow death" at work. We feel as if our hearts have been ripped out. We find no meaning in manual or mental work. Our senses, emotions, and intellect shut down. We're dying. But we can't summon enough energy to revive ourselves.

Rethinking Boredom

Culturally, North America is "bored to death," "bored stiff," "bored to tears," "bored silly," and even "bored out of its skull." People are bored with their marriage partners, school, and sex. They are bored with work, church, prayer, and even television. Surveys indicate that up to half of North Americans are either temporarily or permanently bored,[1] a trend that is all the more disturbing for a society that spends billions of dollars on entertainment and fun.

Boredom begins with having insufficient passion or interest to give ourselves heartily to work and life. It's an absence of feeling that leads to emotional flatness, passivity, and lack of interest in anything or anybody — including God. It alienates us from God, destroys human relationships, and becomes a form of suicide. Therefore, boredom is not so much a sin but a symptom of sin, a sign that our relationship with God, life, and ourselves has been broken. In Romans 1, the apostle Paul writes that the fundamental sin is failure to revere and thank God. From this primal sin come all other sins — including futility (1:21), a variant of boredom.

Boredom can be alleviated by watching a movie, downloading YouTube clips, or seeking some form of mindless amusement. But the great Christian philosopher Søren Kierkegaard considered boredom the pathway to other deadly sins.[2] A classic case of how boredom leads to death can be found in the Bible. One day, King David, who should have been out on the battlefield with his soldiers, found himself at loose ends. He idly watched his neighbor Bathsheba bathe. His bored mind eventually led him down a tangled path of fantasy, lust, adultery, lying, betrayal, and murder.

Not all boredom leads to sin, though. To lapse into daydreaming at work because one is not engaged with the project at that moment is harmless. A short bout of boredom often precedes a fecund and creative period of activity. A little daydreaming could also possibly be a sign of good mental health, since experiencing leisure requires the freedom to move in and out of consciousness. Interestingly enough, people who waited on God often wrestled with boredom. Qoholeth, the brilliant writer of Ecclesiastes who questioned the meaning of life, found that everything was the same "under the sun." The psalmist likened boredom to sorrow that weakens our souls: "My soul melts away with sorrow [boredom]; strengthen me according to your word" (Ps. 119:28). Both Qoholeth and the psalmist concluded that the pursuit of God could overcome the paralysis of boredom.

Boredom at Work

Boredom is not simply an absence of activity. One can be busy and bored at the same time. Rather, boredom results from too little or too much stimulation. We get bored from attending endless meetings, doing repetitive paperwork, and battling office bureaucracy. Boredom strikes when we're trapped in monotonous jobs with limited opportunities to make a difference or to shine.

Bored employees feel their abilities and knowledge aren't valued or harnessed by the organization; they get distracted or demoralized, or they give up hope. Boredom unplugs us from our work and our colleagues. Our work space feels like a prison cell. Even people who have arrived at their corner executive suites might find themselves asking, "Is this all there is to life?"

It's inevitable that work will always have some form of boredom woven into it. Boredom is part of the human predicament, observed the seventeenth-century genius Blaise Pascal, whose creative mind pioneered new discoveries in the fields of mathematics, physics, philosophy, and theology. Said Pascal: "Man is so unhappy that he would be bored even if he had no cause for boredom, by the very nature of his temperament."[3]

Overcoming Boredom

Like many spiritual maladies, our boredom cannot be cured by attacking the problem head on. The journey toward healing from boredom requires, first, humbly acknowledging before God the ways in which we have been wounded by boredom, and then, receiving God's grace. What God offers us, through the Spirit, is peace. Peace gives us a God-given passion for completeness and harmony, no matter what situation we're in. The peace of Christ fills us from within and expels boredom.

Here are some guiding principles on moving from boredom to peace in Jesus Christ:

1. Turn boredom into prayerful waiting. Boredom is an indicator that something has gone awry in our soul life. And it can be virtually impossible to diagnose the roots of boredom and the mysterious desires of our heart. Thus, the need to turn to God in prayer. While waiting can be boring, it can be made contemplative by actively asking God questions with deep longing for insight, as Job did, or by turning to God for strength through hearing the Word of God, as the psalmist did.

65

2. Gain an eternal perspective by keeping the Sabbath. Contrary to the advice of many well-meaning leaders and most parents, the answer to boredom is not simply to work harder. Most bored people need to work less and learn how to keep Sabbath, which is God's deepest provision for an apathetic spirit — one day a week to recover our priorities and celebrate the presence of God. The world offers work and leisure (with no Sabbath); the Bible offers work and Sabbath (with some leisure).

3. Develop a contemplative lifestyle by doing things meaningfully and attending to people, things, and situations in a fuller way that includes their aesthetic and spiritual meaning. We can't subdue boredom by pinning it to the ground. But boredom can be expelled from our hearts — like an unwelcome tenant — when we recover our passion for God. The human predicament, as Kierkegaard said, is a failure to be our (true) selves — creatures in love with God and therefore in love with life.[4] Pascal, out of his own struggle, claimed the answer to boredom lies in an act of faith, or rather a visitation of grace: "Happiness is neither outside us nor inside us; it is in God, both outside and inside us."[5]

Exercise

Reflect on a typical day at work and identify moments or periods of boredom:

- Is the boredom a result of personal factors (your temperament and how you're wired) or the environment (workplace culture or job function)?
- How often do you dream of doing something different? Do you depend on constant excitement or stimulation to keep you alive?

PART TWO

Nine Life-Giving Resources for Workplace Spirituality

Introducing the Spirit's Fruit

Why We Need the Spirit in the Workplace

The Spirit of God's Son has incredible power in breaking sin's stranglehold in the workplace and in the life of the worker. Through the Holy Spirit, our bodies become living receptacles, or "temples," for God's presence (1 Cor 6:19).

The Spirit also battles against the sin embedded deep within us. We receive the Spirit's life-giving resources — love, joy, and peace; patience, kindness, and goodness; gentleness, faithfulness, and self-control — to deploy against the struggles we face as we work. This list of life-giving resources is described as the "fruit of the Spirit" (Gal. 5:22-23).

As we work, we cannot help but produce evil, as evidenced by the nine soul-sapping workplace struggles. But the force of greater good is produced by God's Spirit who lives in us. Evelyn Underhill, a twentieth-century Christian mystic, says that fruits of the Spirit are "ways of thinking, speaking, and acting, which are brought forth in us, gradually but inevitably, by the pressure of Divine Love in our souls."[1] As you can see from the matrix below, the Spirit's fruit transforms our most desperate struggles into joyful outcomes. The Spirit's goodness transforms our greed into gratitude, and God's love transforms our lust into purity.

How do we tap into the Spirit's awesome resources? Not through sheer effort. Most of us have experienced the bitter fail-

Struggles	Fruit	Outcomes
Pride	Joy	Continuous Prayer
Greed	Goodness	Persistent Gratitude
Lust	Love	Beautiful Purity
Gluttony	Self-Control	Joyful Relinquishment
Anger	Gentleness	Surrendered Contentment
Sloth	Faithfulness	Life-Giving Rhythms
Envy	Kindness	Neighbor-Love
Restlessness	Patience	Vocational Confidence
Boredom	Peace	Heavenly-Mindedness

ure of making every effort to get rid of lust, pride, or anger on our own. We don't win our battles against sin that way.

Rather, we come to God by faith and trust. We surrender our minds and our bodies to Jesus Christ. When we do so, we experience the Spirit's resources enabling us to overcome the soul-sapping struggles. Every day, we submit our bodies to God as instruments of righteousness (Rom. 6:13). Specifically, we should:

1. Think and reflect on spiritual attributes (Phil. 4:8)
2. Get rid of vices that hinder the Spirit's work (Eph. 4:31)
3. Make every effort to add virtues to our faith (2 Pet. 1:5)

But remember: we can do these things — thinking of good things, ridding ourselves of sin, and exercising virtue — only by cooperating with God. The nine fruits of the Spirit are gifts. We put these gifts to work by intentionally asking and allowing God to enter our hearts and permeate our work.

The next nine chapters describe how the various fruits of the Spirit serve as life-giving resources for workplace spirituality. They function as an antidote to the poison of the soul-sapping struggles. They remove obstacles that hinder us from working with freedom. They offer us a fresh perspective from which to see God in the workplace. They are new muscles we can exercise and strengthen so that we draw closer to God while we work. Evelyn Underhill says, "Our spiritual life depends on his perpetual coming to us, far more than our going to him."[2]

As we draw on the Spirit's resources, we discover the strength to overcome the nine soul-sapping struggles of the workplace and to live and work as God's agents.

10

Joy: More Than Happiness at Work

Struggle	Fruit	Outcome
Pride Being imprisoned within your self as No. 1	Joy Feeling the exhilaration of having God as No. 1	Continuous Prayer Experiencing continuous communion with God

PS Do you experience joy while you work?

AU I suppose it depends on the work I do. When we went canoeing together on Clearwater Lake, we did a lot of work, paddling the canoe, hour after hour. It can be incredibly repetitive and painfully slow. But as we meandered along the lake shore, I saw an eagle soaring above. I felt the warm glow of the setting sun lighting up the sculptured rocks. There's lots to enjoy if we travel slowly, listening to the dip, dip of the paddles and the drops of water flickering off the blades into the mirror-calm lake.

PS We certainly experienced joy canoeing together, didn't we? But what about joy in the workplace — when we are faced daily with multiple deadlines, an overflowing e-mail in-box and countless meetings?

AU That's exactly my work life. But even in the most stressful situations, I have experienced joy. A short conversation with a colleague can become an opportunity to listen to what God is

doing in her life. Holy and joyful moments happen throughout the day when we share our hopes and struggles — over
lunch or around the water cooler.

PS What you are talking about sounds much more than just being happy at work. There's a fundamental difference between
joy and happiness, isn't there?

AU Yes, you experience joy when you sense God's presence, here
and now.

Rethinking Joy

The hallmark of joy is living responsively to the Spirit no matter
what we're doing in the workplace — sitting through a sales pitch,
dealing with an irate customer, stepping into a difficult board
meeting, or dealing with a colleague who dislikes us. Joy is more
than happiness. Happiness is an emotion — feeling good, having
well-being. But you can have joy even in adverse times. Joy is God-
connection, God-infusion, whole-person exhilaration, blissful
well-being, a spiritual transcendence. Noted Bible teacher William
Barclay says that joy is "the distinguishing atmosphere of the
Christian life."[1] Scripture is full of joy — people who are exhilarated by having God as No. 1 in their lives.

Joy is the alter ego of pride. Pride stems from the energy we
summon to prop up ourselves as No. 1. Joy stems from the energy
we express in worshiping God. Pride strips us of joy; joy strips
away pride.

Joy is not only a personal experience but can be the dominant
atmosphere of a workplace culture. The kingdom of God is righteousness, peace, and joy (Rom. 14:17). The story of God's good
news starts and ends with joy. Joy filled the night sky when the an-
gels proclaimed the birth of Jesus to the shepherds. And one day,
joy will fill the cosmos when the dynamic rule of God is estab-
lished in the new heaven and new earth.

While speaking to his followers about remaining in the love
of God, Jesus said, "I have said these things to you so that my joy
may be in you, and that your joy may be complete" (John 15:11).

71

Far from bringing a person soul-deadening religion, the impact of Jesus on a human life is intoxicating and exhilarating. The highest scriptural endorsement of the spirituality of work is found in Jesus' Parable of the Talents. At the conclusion of the story, the master rewarded two workers who invested their wealth and abilities fruitfully by saying to them, "Enter into the joy of your master" (Matt. 25:23). When we work wholeheartedly, work becomes a means for entering God's presence and enjoying God's joy.

Joy at Work

Dennis Bakke, the former CEO of AES, a U.S.-based energy company, writes in *Joy at Work* that "most people don't believe that fun and work can coexist." He describes a miserable workplace where employees are lazy and work primarily for the money. Workers put their own interests ahead of what is best for the organization; no one wants to be responsible; and employees need to be constantly told what to do.[2] The result: employees want higher pay and better benefits but fewer hours on the job.

Bakke then explains what he did to transform a bureaucratic energy utility into a joyful workplace. He empowered people to use their talents, delegated decisions to the lowest level, built dynamic and fluid teams, created a sense of community, and imparted the knowledge that what one is doing has significant purpose. This sounds an awful lot like management-speak, except that Bakke actually did it. He did redemptive work by engineering the culture of a workplace to become joyful. Bakke didn't do it alone; he did it by cooperating with the Spirit, who wants people to enter into joy.

There is room for joyful creativity in the workplace, no matter how seemingly oppressive things can be. John Ruskin, the nineteenth-century writer, suggested that the masses have no joy in their work and therefore they look to making money as a way of pursuing pleasures outside of their work. It was particularly the joy of making things with one's hands, Ruskin argued, that was

72

lost by the Industrial Revolution.[3] The Information Age and the present Age of Creativity perhaps offer more scope for creativity as work moves from repetitive tasks to creative interventions, a kind of artisanship done in the imagination and mind, though society still needs individually hand-crafted things, as well.

Work that we enjoy doing enables us to use our gifts and talents. We lose all sense of time when we are doing it. We might even daydream about our work when we are not working. But alas, there is no perfect fit this side of heaven. Few people are constantly ecstatic about what they do. And workplace spirituality does not guarantee that frustrating work will become 100 percent fun. (Anyway, experiencing joy at work is more than merely having fun.)

Cultivating the Fruit of Joy

Joy begins when we know why and for whom we work. Most of us work for love, whether we realize it or not. That is, we work to provide for people we love, such as our spouse and children, our neighbors and friends, perhaps even our nation. Love has an endless capacity to transform work into a sacrament of joy.

Ultimately, there is joy in working for God, for God receives our work. In the Parable of the Sheep and Goats, the Lord himself addresses the righteous ones by saying that their work — feeding, clothing, visiting, and welcoming — was work that "you did . . . to me" (Matt. 25:40). It is easy to relegate this text solely to social relief projects. But feeding, clothing, visiting, welcoming, and giving drink to the thirsty are ways of loving our neighbors and supplying their needs. Most of our jobs have the potential to fulfill these roles — if only we have the capacity to see things from God's point of view.

The world is languishing for lack of this kind of joy. The apostle Paul says that joy comes when we keep in step with the Spirit, aligning ourselves with God and God's leading, remaining in God's love, as Jesus said, and keeping the commandment of Jesus — which is simply to love.

73

Exercises

1. Identify specific moments of joy you've encountered over the past week:
   - In what ways did you experience joy working with your colleagues, staff, or customers?
   - In what ways did you experience joy while doing the work itself?
   - What are some things you're grateful for in your organization's systems, processes, and structures? (Examples include health benefits, a robust code of ethics, a meritocratic reward system.)
   - How will you allow yourself to be purposefully exhilarated by joy even when your daily work may be lackluster or just plain difficult?
2. Practice the discipline of thanksgiving by recalling and thanking God for five to ten specific moments that give you joy each day.

11

Goodness: Unselfconscious Giving

Struggle	Fruit	Outcome
Greed Inflaming the passion to possess more than you have	Goodness Cultivating a character that gives rather than takes	Persistent Gratitude Experiencing the freedom of knowing that all you have comes from God

AU You've worked as a pastor, carpenter, dean, and professor. What does it mean, for you, to be doing good work?

PS I've valued doing "the Lord's work" both on the job and in the church. The several years I spent as a carpenter were good because I was doing good work — building and renovating houses. The work fit my gifts and abilities. And I had a sense that I was doing God's work, just as when I was a pastor.

AU And what about when you became an academic dean of Regent College?

PS I had the privilege of hosting a remarkable theological faculty composed of good people. Along the way, I discovered that the seemingly tedious administrative duties could also become a good ministry — I was playing a role in creating an infrastructure and culture in which faculty and staff could thrive.

AU That's a very helpful perspective on how to view the tedious aspects of work. On one hand, I can see my past jobs as a series of relentless projects and gripe about them. Or on the other hand, with the Spirit's creative help, I can see myself doing good work by empowering future leaders and creating environments for their talents to flourish.

PS The wonderful thing is this: as we seek to do good work, God is transforming us into a person of goodness, to be a giver rather than a taker.

Rethinking Goodness

Goodness is a simple word that conveys highly attractive qualities in a person such as integrity, honesty, and uprightness. In contrast to a greedy person, who is inflamed by the passion to possess, a good person is someone who gives rather than takes, who shares rather than hoards. The Greek word for "goodness," *agathosynē*, used by the apostle Paul only three times in the New Testament,[1] conveys true prosperity of life (Eccles. 6:3).

As we seek after the true prosperity of goodness, we are not alone in our quest. The fellowship of the triune God accompanies and empowers us. As we become more aware of the goodwill shared among the Father, Son, and Holy Spirit, we will be transformed. We will aspire to be more and more like Jesus, the perfect human person who walked across the stage of history. Jesus is an immensely attractive person because his goodness transcends justice. With justice people get their due. But with goodness, people desire to give even more. They give *all* that might benefit and help others.[2] Jesus' sacrificial act on the cross — giving us his life — is perhaps the most significant act of goodness in history.

According to an old legend, a bishop who was offered the power to heal declined and asked instead for goodness: "The thing I most desire is that God would bestow upon me the gift of doing a great deal of good without even knowing it myself."[3] In the Christian tradition this goodness has been often been expressed in almsgiving, giving something to relieve the poor.

Goodness at Work

The medieval theologian Thomas Aquinas identified seven corporeal areas of almsgiving, in which good deeds address bodily needs. In the table below, we've suggested modern equivalents of acts of almsgiving in which goodness can be carried out through business and industrial activity:

Seven Areas of Almsgiving

Medieval Acts	Modern Workplaces for Carrying Out These Acts
Feeding the hungry	Food industry, restaurants
Giving drink to the thirsty	Water management, beverage provision
Clothing the naked	Textile and clothing enterprises
Harboring the homeless	Hospitality industry and hotels
Visiting the sick	Medicine, health care, counseling
Ransoming the captive	Law enforcement agencies, military
Burying the dead	Hospice and funeral services

Granted, there is a shadowy and exploitative side to all the modern businesses listed above. Nonetheless, a lot of good has been done — and is being carried out — through business and human enterprise in the twenty-first century.

Aquinas also addressed the seven spiritual deeds for almsgiving: to instruct the ignorant, to counsel the doubtful, to comfort the sorrowful, to reprove the sinner, to forgive injuries, to bear with those who trouble and annoy us, and to pray for all.[4] These are the inner dispositions that we can adopt as we work and relate with our colleagues every day.

A powerful form of almsgiving sweeping the world in the past decade is expressed through microfinance, which provides credit, savings, and insurance services to poor or low-income clients. Centuries ago, the medieval Jewish mystic Maimonides (1135-1204) had already contended, in what is called the Ladder of Charitable Giving, that creating new wealth for the poor is the highest degree of charity. The steps on the ladder are:

1. A person gives, but only when asked by the poor.
2. A person gives, but is glum when giving.
3. A person gives cheerfully, but less than he or she should.
4. A person gives without being asked, but gives directly to the poor. Now the poor know who gave them help and the giver, too, knows whom he or she has benefited.
5. A person throws money into the house of someone who is poor. The poor person does not know to whom he or she is indebted, but the donor knows who has been helped.
6. A person gives a donation in a certain place and then turns his or her back in order not to know which of the poor has been helped, but the poor person knows to whom he or she is indebted.
7. A person gives anonymously to a fund for the poor. Here the poor person does not know to whom he or she is indebted, and the donor does not know who has been helped. But, the highest is this:
8. Money is given to prevent another from becoming poor, such as providing him or her with a job, or teaching the person a trade, or setting up the person in business. Thus, the recipient will not be forced to the dreadful alternative of holding out a hand for charity. This is the highest step and the summit of charity's golden ladder.[5]

Cultivating the Fruit of Goodness

Good people enrich others. In doing so, and often without realizing it, they find real wealth — prosperity in God. The contrary is also true. Jesus tells the story of a rich entrepreneur whose crops yielded an incredible profit. So he planned to build bigger barns, stop work, and revel in food, drink, and sensual pleasure. The rich man was the antithesis of an almsgiver. God assessed the man's

78

work as failure. "'You fool! This very night your life is being demanded of you.' So it is with those who store up treasures for themselves but are not rich towards God" (Luke 12:20-21).

Jesus poses a challenging question: What does it mean to be rich towards God? We suggest the following:

1. Invest in the kingdom of God (Matt. 6:19-21; Luke 12:31). The kingdom of God is not *just* spiritual. It involves the active rule of God that encompasses spiritual, personal, social, political, and economic dimensions. Kingdom work creates new wealth, alleviates poverty, brings well-being to people, embellishes and improves human life, and battles against organizational structures propped up by greed. We don't have to do "Christian work" or serve in Christian NGOs to invest in the kingdom of God. Any good work, motivated by love of God and neighbor, is kingdom work.

2. Embrace the purpose of God. Human beings are invited to share in God's work. Because God is creator, sustainer, and redeemer, and because God is also provider, judge, instructor, revealer, covenant-maker, and community-builder, we can join God as coworkers in a wonderful variety of work, from agriculture to genetic engineering, from homemaking to journalism. What makes work "Christian" is not the religious character of the work but the fact that we perform the work with faith, hope, and love.

3. Treasure the priorities of God. In Luke 16 Jesus tells a story of a manager about to lose his job. This manager shrewdly goes to all his boss's debtors and negotiates outrageous reductions in their debts. This endears the manager so much to the debtors that when he is sacked, they welcome him into their homes as their friend. "Use worldly wealth to gain friends for yourselves, so that when it is gone, you will be welcomed into eternal dwellings," says Jesus (16:9[TNIV]). Jesus is not encouraging deceitful "buying" of friendship. Rather, he calls us to use our money in ways that build lifelong friendships. The one treasure we can take from this life to the next is the relationships we have made through Christ.

4. Hunger for the presence of God. We are to love God over all competing loves, treasuring God more than anything else. Like the psalmist we proclaim that God is our portion, our treasure, our all in all. "Give thanks to the LORD, for he is good; his steadfast love endures forever" (Ps. 118:1).

So being rich toward God does not mean we stop working. Being rich toward God is embracing the Spirit's gift of goodness that transforms our ordinary work into something beautiful.

Exercises

1. Spend some time in prayerful reflection, asking God to illuminate specific and creative ways in which you can be rich toward God by:

   • Investing in the kingdom of God
   • Embracing the purpose of God
   • Treasuring the priorities of God
   • Hungering for the presence of God

2. In light of these ideas, how can you express goodness in your workplace during the coming week? What are some acts of spiritual almsgiving (such as instructing the ignorant, forgiving injuries, and praying for all) that you could put into practice? Specify the names of people you want to bless.

12

Love: The Greatest Thing to Give and Receive

Struggle	Fruit	Outcome
Lust Imagining how people can be used for self-interest	Love Practically caring for the best interests of others	Beautiful Purity Experiencing whole-hearted love for God and neighbor

PS   Love is probably the most potent and life-giving force in the workplace. Yet few leadership and management gurus talk or write about love.

AU   People fear showing love in a dog-eat-dog world. One evening, I overcame that fear and asked a colleague for advice on a stressful situation. I told him I was on the verge of drowning. He gave lots of advice and volunteered to help me, which I accepted with gratitude. Just as I got up to leave, he asked me if I knew anybody who provided help to drug addicts. He said his daughter had been arrested by the police and tested positive for drugs. Tears rimmed his eyes. He felt he'd failed as a father. "I don't know what to do, but I'm willing to do anything to help my daughter," he said. At that moment, I felt God's loving presence with us. My colleague and I were openly bearing one another's burdens. My colleague demonstrated love by taking time to listen and provide astute advice.

And I sought to love my colleague by supporting him in his personal pain.

PS You were giving and receiving love toward one another.

AU Yes, I discovered that loving one another is never a sign of weakness.

PS Indeed. By loving God's people, we are loving God.

Rethinking Love

We long to love and be loved. As parents, we aspire to love our children. And we rejoice when our children receive our love. It is a universal human longing to perfectly give and receive love. Love, or *caritas,* is the will to do good for the other.

For people of faith, it is also a universal human desire to be loved by God and to love God. The tradition of Christian spirituality notes that God is "lover, the beloved, and the love itself." That is, love is not just an attribute of God. Love is who God is, and love is what God does.[1] Because of this, two corollaries are true:

1. Almighty God, the master of the universe, longs for us to love him as children love a wonderful father, said the Venerable Bede, the seventh-century Benedictine monk and doctor of the church. "It would be no small thing if we were able to love God in the way that a servant loves his master or a worker his employer. But loving God as father is much greater still."[2]

2. We are deeply loved by God. So it is not surprising that in listing the fruit of the Spirit, the apostle Paul started with love. The list is a progressive series with God's love as the crucial starting point. The English Christian mystic Evelyn Underhill says, "Love is . . . that tender, cherishing attitude; that unlimited self-forgetfulness, generosity, and kindness which is the attitude of God to all his creatures."[3]

As noted in chapter 3, our soul-sapping struggle with lust indicates that we long for relationships that are deeper and more real. We long for God's intimate, pure, and chaste love to work in our lives and transform us from within — making us loving people. "The first-fruit of his indwelling presence, the first sign that we are on his side and he on ours, must be at least a tiny bud of this Charity breaking the hard and rigid outline of our life," says Underhill.[4]

Love at Work

In the workplace, we give the most powerful evidence that we are loved by God when we show practical care for the best interests of others. Lust looks to be serviced; love serves.

Consider the following personal evaluation of how you are demonstrating love in action during the daily routine of work. (The questions are based on 1 Corinthians 13, adapted for the workplace.)

- Are you willing to do small things, even when no one is watching?
- Do you look out for opportunities to show kindness to people who are usually ignored, shunned, or overlooked?
- Do you rejoice with the successes of your colleagues and peers?
- Do you resist the temptation to draw attention to yourself?
- Do you treat everyone with respect and courtesy?
- Do you actively choose not to provoke other people?
- Do you consciously choose to frame things in a positive manner, giving your colleagues the benefit of the doubt (while not being blind to their foibles)?
- Do you restrain yourself from inflating other people's faults or exposing their weaknesses in order to tear them down?

In reviewing these questions, you may feel that loving people is not something that comes naturally, especially in the workplace. Possibly, this is because we have ceased to regard our colleagues as people. Large corporations tend to dehumanize employees into units of productivity (labeling people as human resources or capital). We cannot love units of productivity; we can only love people. So how do we receive God's love as we work?

Cultivating the Fruit of Love

God, through the Holy Spirit, pours out love into our hearts if we are willing recipients of God's love. Below are two disciplines that have transformed the hearts and minds of great Christian servants and leaders over the centuries, enabling them to become living receptacles and conduits of God's love.

1. *Form covenantal relationships with the people you work with.* Biblical love is best characterized by *hesed,* a Hebrew word that describes a relationship so faithful, so kind, and so compassionate that it's called a covenant. This covenantal relationship transcends the call of duty. Quite often, the relationship is sparked when one person is spurred to do something — entirely voluntarily — for another person in a time of real need. Over time both people demonstrate abiding loyalty and commitment toward one another. It's a friendship that seeks the good of the other. Covenantal relationships require us to become attentive to people who are shunned (for instance, because of the "wrong" education, race, or background). We focus on developing others for their sakes. We seek creative ways to generate enthusiasm rather than fear. In short, we seek to love people as they are, made in God's image. The best example of intertwined *hesed* relationships can be gleaned from the book of Ruth in the Hebrew Scriptures.[5]

2. *Contemplate Jesus' working relationship with his Father.* The best working relationship in history is the loving relationship between Jesus and his Father. "No other source, whether inside or outside of religions, even comes close to what God in Christ shows of love," says Christian philosopher Dallas Willard.[6] In his three years of active ministry in Palestine, Jesus exemplified for us how to work with the Creator. The Gospel

of John offers a rich treasury of how Jesus worked to do his Father's will. First, Jesus declared that the ultimate goal of his work was to reveal his Father's love and glory. Then, Jesus carried out his work in a number of ways: by loving the people he met in daily life; by loving his Father in private prayer; and by living within the limitations of his human frame.

By contemplating the relationship of Creator and Son, we receive the Spirit's resources for loving our jobs, our colleagues, bosses, subordinates, and even the company itself, with its systems, structures, and culture. We begin to love the things related to work, from pens to photocopy machines, seeing these as tools for God's use. At the same time, working with love requires us to struggle against unjust or evil practices embedded within the organization's systems and culture. Not least, as we come to love the things and people that God loves, we begin to love our selves deeply (not selfishly) in the same way that Jesus Christ loves us.

Exercise

By contemplating Jesus' working relationship with his Father in the Gospel of John, we can derive guiding principles and attitudes applicable to the workplace. Below is a list of mind-sets (by no means exhaustive) that we could adopt while working. Pick one mind-set that challenges or inspires you and bring it alive in your workplace for as long as you think is necessary.

1. I am an agent of the living God sent to bring faith, hope, and love into the marketplace. Just as the Creator sent Jesus to be with us, God has sent me into the workplace. I am God's Sent One.
2. Apart from God, I can do nothing. Without God, I have no energy, creativity, or initiative.
3. With God, I have limitless resources to draw on, working with power and glory, pointing people to Jesus.
4. I can do only what God does — nothing more, nothing less.

5. I choose to do work that has enduring value.
6. I choose to avoid work that has no eternal value.
7. My work is a gift from God.
8. My work is done to glorify God.
9. I relinquish my own will in order to do God's will.
10. The work God calls me to do is always good — no matter how dry or difficult.
11. I shall be responsive to God's slightest touch and guidance.
12. I am loved by God, who is deeply pleased with me.

13

Self-Control: Resolving the Work-Life Dilemma

Struggle	Fruit	Outcome
Gluttony Looking for satisfaction through excessive consumption	Self-Control Being governed by godly living and the Spirit's leading	Joyful Relinquishment Experiencing the freedom to release a preoccupation with food and to eat more simply

AU Some days, my colleagues and I are convinced that we can't go on like this — working too much, doing too much, maybe eating too much. It's a crazy lifestyle — constantly spiraling out of control.

PS Edward Hallowell, a Harvard psychiatrist, calls this "attention deficit trait." ADT is caused by a hyperkinetic environment, when workplace pressure increases and people "suck it up" without complaining. ADT people multitask obsessively, answer questions in superficial ways, hurry all the time, spend little or no time with friends, work longer hours, and sleep less. ADT people find it difficult to generate fresh ideas.

AU How do you refill that empty tank?

PS Hallowell says that ADT can be controlled by re-engineering one's work environment to create "human moments" — getting enough sleep, exercising, and switching to a good diet.[1]

AU   Sounds like Work-Life Balance 101! And yet most of us struggle to find that balance. It's not as easy as it sounds.

PS   Indeed. The antidote to a crazy lifestyle is not striving for
more work-life balance. Rather, it is cultivating self-control.

Rethinking Self-Control

We long for equilibrium in life so we can oscillate between activity
and rest, work and play, engagement with people and personal
time for reflection. This pursuit seems tantalizingly elusive,
though, in view of the craziness of modern life.

More people across the board — from entry level to senior
management — are experiencing burnout due to overwork and
stress. Time for family, meaningful conversation, leisure, creative
hobbies, and church has vanished. The proliferation of e-mail, cell
phones, laptops, and Blackberries has increased our work hours
and reduced our access to privacy and silence. A recent American
survey conducted by the Center for Work-Life Policy indicates
that eight out of ten people say their jobs are affecting their
health.[2] The *New York Times* reported that sixty-two percent of
survey respondents say their workload has increased over the last
six months, while more than half say work leaves them overtired
and overwhelmed.[3]

Not all of the pressures are external; sometimes we are the
cause of our own drivenness and misery. A Christian executive of
a multinational corporation said that on Sunday he ranked God,
family, and work as his top three concerns in order of priority. On
Monday, however, he admitted that the order shifted to work,
family, and only then God. Tragically, this downward spiral stems
from the desire to have it all — a great job, a fat salary, well-
educated children, five-star-rated vacations, the latest gadgets,
and a vibrant religious life.

In contrast to the gluttonous urge to milk the most out of life,
the gift of self-control granted by the Holy Spirit nourishes and
governs the inner person — giving us control over our actions
and appetites. With self-control, we no longer try to find satisfac-

tion from excesses or the drive to have it all. Self-control helps us find satisfaction in God, accepting whatever God gives us.

The infusion of God's grace through the indwelling Spirit results in self-control *(egkrateia)*. Self-control gives us the inner strength of restraint, or the ability to have a grip on one's self. The apostle Peter exhorts his readers to "make every effort to add to your faith goodness; and to goodness, knowledge; and to knowledge, self-control" (2 Pet. 1:5-6). The effort we exert is not to attain self-mastery, but to cooperate with God and to seek God's help. God graciously grants us self-control, or the ability to exercise self-denial, in order to quell the human impulse to sin. The writer of Proverbs likens the soul of a person without self-control to a city that cannot defend against enemy attacks because the walls have crumbled (Prov. 25:28). That is exactly what happens if we exercise no restraint over our passions. Self-control functions as a robust door that guards our soul and prevents the minions of anger, lust, gluttony, and other deadly sins from overwhelming us.

Self-Control at Work

Jesus of Nazareth is the exemplar of self-control at work, although he did not set out to achieve work-life balance. At times, Jesus was so engaged in service that he did not have time to eat. Widows, the demon-possessed, and anxious parents petitioned him to wield miraculous power. Because of his compassion for people, Jesus was besieged by the fierce urgency of *now*. And yet he lived a disciplined, self-controlled life. Surrounded by a crowd that made demands that only the savior of the world could meet, Jesus at times "dismissed the crowd" (Mark 6:45). This required inner strength. Jesus could have been tempted to heal more and more people. But mindful of his mission, Jesus probably had to say: "I can't heal you right now, I'm sorry. I must be alone with my Father." That is the paradigm of self-control — doing the right thing at the right time to draw close to God.

We see current workplace attempts to seek self-control in the pursuit of a "work-life balance," that is, by juggling the demands of work and personal life. Proponents of work-life balance propose that we keep a log, explore flex hours and job-sharing, say no, seek domestic help, practice yoga or meditation, prioritize leisure time, get enough sleep, or seek out professional help. Ironically, the quest to achieve work-life balance often makes us feel even more scattered and dissatisfied. It's entirely possible that seeking work-life balance can become a form of excessive consumption — the desire to have it all and to be able to juggle as many balls as possible. This has led John Dalla Costa, a Canadian business consultant, to conclude that "balance is bunk."[4]

When we practice self-control we can say no and yes with integrity, no to one more assignment that will lead to work overload, and yes to an assignment we can do with passion and competence. We will be able to leave the workplace with unfinished business, knowing that God never requires us to do more than God gives us time in which to do it. We will give not just "quality time" to our families and friends — as though this kind of time can be organized or prearranged — but also "quantity time." (In passing we note that quality time of focused and deep interaction happens when we are "hanging out" with people and are sensitive to the leading of the Spirit.) When we have self-control, we can give ourselves to an exercise program or to an enriching hobby without feeling guilty.

Ultimately, dealing with a life spiraling out of control is a spiritual discipline. We must allow ourselves to be led by the Spirit who produces the fruit of self-control in us. Self-control enables us to be governed from the inside through values that are aligned with God's. A person with self-control learns to respond to the Spirit's leading. Instead of practicing a gluttonous lifestyle, where we seek to have it all, self-control enables us to live in alignment with godly principles. Instead of the modern pursuit of work-life balance, the apostle Paul prayed that we "may be strengthened in [our] inner being with power through his Spirit, and that Christ may dwell in [our] hearts through faith" (Eph. 3:16-17).

In other words, it is the Spirit who gives us self-control in dealing with work addiction and the overwhelming pressures of contemporary life. Self-control is better than balance, more attainable, and maybe even more desirable. Balance is about doing everything in moderation and living a completely composed life with all our priorities lined up like ducks in a row and worked out in calculated precision like a sequenced computer program. Nothing disturbs the perfectly balanced person. Such is not the quality of a person whose heart is lined up with our passionate God. The great saints did not live balanced lives, nor did the prophets. They filled their days with white-hot passion, enflamed by a mighty cause. The apostle Paul spoke about working with "all the energy that [Christ] so powerfully inspires in me" (Col. 1:29).

Cultivating the Fruit of Self-Control

There is a better way than struggling to attain balance through time management and breaking down one's life into a series of action items. The better way comes through viewing all of life as sacred. We may never live the balanced life. But we can make every effort to seek God's help. In doing so, we gradually gain self-control. How do we begin this journey? We propose three steps.

1. Identify the areas where you might lack self-control:
    *   What are your cravings?
    *   What things do you believe you truly need?
    *   What do you think, dream, or fantasize about in your spare time?
    *   What do you cling to or fear letting go?
    *   What are the areas in life that give you a sense of security?
    *   Are any of the things you listed above more important than God?

    Note: By answering the questions with specificity, you will be able to confess any sinful preoccupations to God.
2. Specify the priorities in your life. Do not list them out as bullet points but sketch them out as an interdependent web of essentials. For instance, your priorities might include family, work, rest, sleep, service, church, social responsibility, citizenship, and personal recreation. Place God at the center of this

web — not at the top of a list. This helps you see that God is central to work, family, church, and everything else. Note that we are not placing "religious life" (for instance, church attendance, quiet times, and witnessing) at the center. Rather, God must be at the center, because God is in all things.

3. Put into practice some spiritual disciplines that will allow the Spirit to control your life:
   - The daily discipline of ongoing relinquishment: Find several creative ways to release possessions in order to live and work more simply — such as limiting the number of electronic gadgets you own or dropping subscriptions to magazines you don't read and services you don't use.
   - The daily discipline of walking through the narrow gate: Renounce the mindless approach to life by which you walk through a broad, easy gate. Rather, choose the way of the cross — following Jesus into difficult but life-giving places, which requires sacrifice (Matt. 7:14).
   - The daily discipline of keeping company with Jesus Christ: Establish as your ultimate life goal having Jesus always before and behind you. Try to draw closer to him daily, until your dying breath. If you do this, your life will unselfconsciously become governed by self-control.

Exercise

Review the questions, suggestions, and spiritual disciplines on cultivating self-control. Share what you've learned with a friend this week and choose one thing you'd like to put into practice. Ask your friend to check in regularly with you for a month.

14

Gentleness: The Strength of Meekness

Struggle	Fruit	Outcome
Anger Using passion to manipu- late and control people and circumstances	Gentleness Empowering others by renouncing personal agendas and expressing meekness	Surrendered Contentment Experiencing the satis- faction of who you are, what you have, and what you do

PS   In a highly competitive workplace, a crucial management skill is the ability to get things done. Would it be seen as a sign of weakness if you were not able to push through your own agenda?

AU   I think there is nothing wrong with getting people to buy into my agenda, especially if the agenda is aligned with God's values and the corporation's highest aspirations. Being assertive sometimes can be a good thing.

PS   Does that mean that the spirit of gentleness has no place in the workplace?

AU   It's certainly rare. On one occasion, I was roped in by two bosses to prepare for a potentially explosive meeting. Just in case things went wrong, they wanted to ensure that none of our heads rolled. So we brainstormed tactics. At one point, the two bosses suggested a good-cop-bad-cop routine. One of them said, "Let's get Alvin to play the bad cop. He could spread the blame around." But the other boss quickly replied, "There's no way this will work. Alvin would never do it. He'd never tear down other people's reputations. He's too much of a gentleman."

PS It must be gratifying to be known as a person who refuses to backbite or blame others.

AU Yes, I felt grateful. That's one occasion when it felt good to be considered a "gentle" man!

Rethinking Gentleness

In a high-performance organization, the stereotypical gentle manager is like a speck of dust in one's eye — inconsequential yet irritating to the body politic. He or she would be obsequious, groveling, weak, probably passive-aggressive. In contrast, we admire leaders who are hard-charging, Type A personalities such as "Neutron Jack" Welch, former CEO of General Electric. It seems as if gentleness has no place in today's hyper-competitive workplace. And yet perhaps it is in the shark-infested waters of the business world that the godly qualities of gentleness are most needed.

The Greek word for gentleness or meekness is *praÿtēs*. Gentleness is a fruit of the Spirit, and the Greek word for it also describes a powerful animal that has learned to accept discipline, such as a bridled horse, which generates tremendous speed and power at the rider's bidding, or a dog that's fierce toward strangers but friendly toward the master's children. Similarly, the Bible describes a gentle soul as one whose quiet but firm disposition in dealing with people reflects the willingness to surrender one's desires and disposition to God.

Moses is one such example and was called "the meekest man on earth" (Num. 12:3), precisely because he allowed Yahweh to guide his every step. He rose from a stuttering shepherd to become a prophet-political leader. Millennia later, the Lord Jesus Christ, the new Moses, described himself as "meek and gentle."

94

The apostle Paul subsequently identified a gentle spirit as a key attribute to help Christian leaders flourish in hostile circumstances. Note that Moses, Jesus, and Paul were no pushovers: they were tough. In facing overwhelming odds and bitter rivals, they responded with a most uncommon grace, by being gentle souls. Paul observed that God's elect clothe themselves in meekness (Col. 3:12). He exhorted Christians to let their gentleness be evident to all (Phil. 4:5). (This exhortation to be gentle appears in the Bible at least two dozen times.)[1]

As such, gentleness and meekness are highly valued attributes in Christian spirituality. These qualities describe courageous and disciplined people with nerves of steel. Gentleness is the conduit for harnessing strength and power. It serves as a tiller for a three-thousand-horsepower tugboat surging along a river. A gentle person is an individual of great power who has restrained his or her strength for the good of the weaker one. A wise action or word, carried out judiciously and timed perfectly, can inspire change even in the toughest or most complicated situation. "A soft tongue can break bones," observes the writer of Proverbs (25:15).

Gentleness at Work

The entire life of our Lord Jesus embodies gentleness. He is our role model for becoming gentle souls in the workplace. "Learn from me, for I am gentle and humble in heart," Jesus said (Matt. 11:29). Jesus' disciple, Matthew, later concluded that Jesus' attitudes and actions corresponded with the suffering servant in Isaiah who submitted his will to God. "He will not break a bruised reed or quench a smoldering wick until he brings justice to victory" (Matt. 12:20, quoting Isa. 42:3). Jesus deals gently with people on the verge of falling apart. He reconciles and strengthens the weak and the suffering. Jesus inspires people to change; repentant people who encounter him never walk away in despair.

Such gentleness requires a profound respect for the personal dignity of the other. A gentle person studiously avoids any coercion, intimidation, or threats. If possible, he or she might seek to change a wrong attitude through a kind act or persuasive word, but a gentle person will refuse to force his or her hand against the other person's will. A gentle person seeks to move at the pace of another person's readiness to make changes or embrace a goal. This is exactly the kind of person you'd like to have as your boss or leader. Self-assured, he or she empowers you in a way that's best suited for your needs.

As you reflect on your working life, consider the questions below as indicators of the Spirit's gentle work in your life in the workplace:

- Do you allow subordinates to make mistakes, and when they do, do you treat them in a firm yet compassionate manner?
- Do you show equal respect in the way you speak to the secretary or lunchroom worker and to the CEO?
- Do you delight in serving others?
- Do you respond to the slightest touch of the Spirit, or do you require heavy discipline before coming to your senses?
- Are you aware of what you do not know, so that you are willing to receive instruction with meekness and a teachable spirit?
- Do you choose to listen and build relationships with your opponent, boss, staff, and negotiating partner, no matter how difficult they are? Or do you browbeat them into submission by ramming ideas down their throats?
- Are you able to rebuke without anger? Argue without being dismissive? Treat everyone with complete courtesy?
- When you correct someone or provide feedback, do you give him or her hope and greater determination for excellence? Or does the person become discouraged or driven to despair?

Cultivating the Fruit of Gentleness

We do not become gentle souls on our own. Gentleness is part of the fruit of the Spirit. When we rest secure in knowing that we are strong, we do not need to be pushy or arrogant. We do not fight or exhibit a belligerent or pugnacious spirit. What a contrast this is to people who amass the symbols of power, money, and reputation as a show of strength (though inwardly they probably feel feeble).

On a deeper level, gentle people have gone through these steps: surrender, renunciation, obedience, and subservience. They have the willingness to be molded. This willingness to give up power produces radical change in the way we treat others. Paul tells Titus to "be ready for every good work, . . . and to be gentle . . . to everyone" (Titus 3:1-2). This requires bearing wrong done to you, yet remaining willing to help others.[2]

What do gentle souls do or not do?

- People who are gentle do not wound others with rash words or cold disregard.
- They acknowledge their vulnerability to sin and weakness. This enables them to empathize deeply with other people's struggles.
- They respond with "gentleness and reverence" (1 Pet. 3:15) when faced off against people who mock, ridicule, or dismiss them.
- They do not give in or buckle under pressure, especially when ethical principles are compromised. They might appear to be weak. But their goal is actually to reconcile people to God and with each other.
- They are not paralyzed or overwhelmed when confronted with other people's pain. This is because they, too, have learned what it means to endure pain and to joyfully accept daily crosses as gifts from God.

When we choose the path of gentleness, we find freedom for ourselves, as we discover the reality of a gentle God who loves us. We are like a spring of water or a source of refreshment for people who meet us. Amma Syncletica, a wise Egyptian desert mother, said: "Choose the meekness of Moses and you will find your heart which is a rock changed into a spring of water."[3]

Exercise

Gary Thomas, a writer and founder of the Center for Evangelical Spirituality, suggests three steps toward cultivating a spirit of gentleness.[4]

1. Consider Jesus' gentleness (Isa. 40:11; 42:3; 1 Pet. 2:23). What enabled Jesus to endure the harshest treatment without retaliating (when he very well could have)?
2. Be gentle toward yourself. How are you inclined to feel about yourself when you fall short of perfection? Circle all of the following words that apply (and add any additional words that come to mind):
   - angry
   - ashamed
   - disgusted
   - amused
   - pessimistic
   - frustrated
   - forgiving
   - accepting
   - embarrassed
   - resigned
   - confident
   - sad

   How did Jesus respond to the people in the following passages (Luke 7:36-50; 19:1-10; 23:39-43), all of whom had failed in some way?
3. Be gentle toward others. How do you usually respond when someone lets you down? Summarize what the following verses say about showing gentleness to others (1 Thess. 2:7; 1 Tim. 6:11; 2 Tim. 2:24-25; 1 Pet. 3:8-9; 3:15). Do you know someone who needs a touch of Jesus' gentleness in his or her life? How can you be a channel of gentleness to that person?

15

Faithfulness: Workplace Integrity

Struggle	Fruit	Outcome
Sloth Doing minimal or the least important work and loving ease	Faithfulness Persisting in important work with utter reliability	Life-Giving Rhythms Experiencing a pattern of life that produces excellent work without being consumed by it

AU Paul, you've taken on many challenging projects that don't yield immediate results. What helps you to work wholeheartedly and faithfully when things get difficult?

PS When I left pastoral work for carpentry, I learned there was much more to becoming a skilled artisan than merely tinkering on woodworking projects. The biggest challenge my boss and I faced was in finishing the projects we'd started. We found it much easier to start new projects, but it took us ages to do the finishing touches, which meant it took us ages before we got paid! That's when I learned the importance of being reliable and developed the ability to persist to the end. I was eventually rewarded with a partnership in the company.

AU That was quite a switch in jobs, from pastor to carpenter. What did you discover in doing something that was completely different?

PS I discovered that most jobs are open only to candidates with years of relevant experience. That approach is wrong. Dee Hock, President of Visa International, argues that we should "hire and promote first on the basis of integrity; second, motivation; third, capacity; fourth, understanding; fifth, knowledge; and last and least, experience." He says that "without integrity, motivation is dangerous; without motivation, capacity is impotent; without capacity, understanding is limited; without understanding, knowledge is meaningless; without knowledge, experience is blind. Experience is easy to provide and quickly put to use by people with the other qualities."[1]

AU Some companies I've worked with seem to think that money is the best motivating force in spurring productivity.

PS Definitely not. Money motivates neither the best people nor the best in people. The key is spending most of your time managing yourself — your ethics, character, principles, purpose, motivation, and conduct.

Rethinking Faithfulness

Faithful people are highly valued in the workplace. Their word is trustworthy. Work gets done even when nobody's watching. When people are watching, faithful workers have nothing to hide. They accomplish tasks in a single-minded manner. They may not necessarily be superstars in the company. And sometimes, they may balk at taking on new challenges — not because they are bone-lazy but because they need to be convinced that the work is important enough and that they can deliver on their promises. They are trustworthy. Faithful people are marked by integrity.

The Greek word *pistos* describes a person whose faithful service is reliable and dependable.[2] Jesus Christ is the perfect embodiment of the faithful worker. He demonstrated this by becoming the faithful high priest who accomplished his atoning work on the cross, forgave our sins, and brought us into God's presence. Theologian William Barclay contends that Jesus' faithfulness was so exemplary that not only can humanity depend on Jesus, "but God also can depend on Jesus."[3]

In receiving the fruit of the Spirit, we are receiving the character of God who is faithful. The more we rely on God, the more faithful we become. This quality of fidelity is what we look for in servants (Titus 2:10).

Faithfulness at Work

Faithfulness gets expressed in the workplace primarily through integrity. A person of integrity demonstrates consistency between inner and outer lives and between word and deed. A person who acts with integrity becomes dependable and reliable and, therefore, faithful. Such a person leads a transparent life.

Integrity, therefore, is a synonym for faithfulness. Stephen L. Carter, a professor at Yale Law School, defines integrity as the ability to:

1. Discern what is right and wrong
2. Act on what has been discerned, even at personal cost
3. Speak openly about one's understanding of right and wrong.[4]

In Deuteronomy 17:15-20, God describes the attributes of a king whose rule is marked by integrity. The integrity and faithfulness of the king — or any leader — need to be worked out in six different areas:

1. Social integrity: "One of your own community you may set as king over you" (Deut. 17:15). No one can influence the system without participating wholeheartedly in it. This advice is often not heeded, however, in the search to appoint new executives or pastors.
2. Financial integrity: "He must not acquire many horses for himself . . . also silver and gold he must not acquire in great quantity for himself" (Deut. 17:16, 17). Today, CEOs have no qualms about being paid two or three hundred times the sal-

ary of entry-level employees. Many business and political leaders have also fleeced stockholders and citizens. People without financial integrity cannot work with faithfulness.

3. Directional integrity: The king must lead people in the right direction and not take them back to Egypt (see Deut. 17:16). In the same way, leaders must be faithful in casting a vision — articulating a destiny and hope that points to greater trust in God rather than retreating to the security of the "tried and true" trust in one's own abilities.

4. Sexual integrity: "He must not acquire many wives for himself, or else his heart will turn away" (Deut. 17:17). One of the most common areas where leaders fall is in the area of sexual fidelity. Inflated by pride and bored by the mundane, they seek new thrills that undermine their trustworthiness and faithfulness to people.

5. Moral integrity: The morals of the king are bound to a higher authority. "He shall have a copy of this law written for him. . . . It shall remain with him and he shall read it all the days of his life" (Deut. 17:18). Without a moral conscience shaped by God, people become unmoored and lack the faithfulness to persist in important tasks.

6. Relational integrity: He must not "exalt himself above other members of the community" (Deut. 17:20). Herein lies the greatest challenge — for a high-ranking person to regard him- or herself as no better than others. Personal humility and meekness must characterize the leader, or for that matter, any person who follows God.

Cultivating the Fruit of Faithfulness

The workplace is the crucible where we discover our deep need of God; in other words, we come to know ourselves as needy, hungry, and longing for God to transform our character. We would not be able to become faithful workers without God's help. The first step in seeking God's help is to discern the areas in which we need to grow in faithfulness. We can do three things:

1. Ask for feedback: Seek out feedback from colleagues for areas of growth. Listen carefully to any criticism without trying to explain yourself. Criticism, whether true or not, is valuable in revealing any inconsistencies within yourself.

2. Consider a specific occasion when you have let someone down: what happened? What were the circumstances that led you to become unfaithful to that relationship?

3. Reflect on any failure you've experience due to your performance at work. Was it an issue of integrity related to any of the six areas of kingly integrity listed above?

While the questions and exercises above might appear too introspective, they are life-giving because they help us gain greater knowledge of our divided selves. "Without external work we could not know ourselves fully, for only in daily work do we have a perfect opportunity to observe ourselves; it is then indeed that we discover the good and evil in ourselves, and see our merits and faults," notes Polish Cardinal Wyszyński.[5] As our Achilles' heel is exposed, we become more ready to come before God in a posture of surrender, humbly seeking help in our efforts to become faithful servants.

In your prayers, you could also ask God for the tenacity and courage to:

1. Invite a colleague or friend to become an accountability partner: In your dealings with him or her, go the extra mile in sharing your weaknesses. Give your friend the license to relentlessly follow through to ensure that you are keeping your word.

2. Obey God promptly: When you sense the Spirit's gentle and quiet promptings, do not delay. Do not boast about your action but do it cheerfully — and with great love.

3. Choose one small area to grow in faithfulness: Identify a specific area in your life or a specific task entrusted to you in the workplace. As you learn to be faithful in that one small area, you will also become faithful in bigger things. At the very least, you would be safeguarding yourself from over-promising and under-delivering.

Exercises

1. Review the steps and ideas for cultivating the fruit of faithfulness. Choose the most significant area and ask for God's own character to be revealed in you.

2. Review the six areas of integrity required in a leader and determine which area in your life needs the Spirit's fresh infusion. Write down a few necessary goals (short- to long-term) that will help you become a faithful worker. Display this list prominently (for instance, on your bathroom mirror) as a daily reminder.

16

Kindness: Putting Others at Ease

Struggle	Fruit	Outcome
Envy Feeling pain because of someone else's advancement and possessions	Kindness Putting others at ease by rejoicing in their gifts and achievements	Neighbor–Love Experiencing the ability to meet the needs of others and to contribute to their well-being

AU This might sound like a naïve question. But what would it look like if leaders in business, politics, and Christian organizations treated one another with kindness?

PS It might look like my father, the president of a steel company, who embodied kindness. Every summer, I worked in a different division in the company — punch presses, warehouse, shipping, payroll, and filing. It gave me the opportunity to observe my father at work. His office door was always open. All day, a stream of people came in and went out. He welcomed people, listened to them, put them at ease. He forgave people who made mistakes. Long after Dad had retired, my cousin met the sweeper who had worked for my father. This man said that Ernest Stevens treated him with dignity and made him feel important.

AU The story of your father shows that true hospitality — or demonstrating kindness — cannot be done for show. It cannot be engineered into a system or process. Kindness in action is a matter of the heart.

PS   Yes. I've been deeply challenged by the words of Jean Vanier, who founded L'Arche communities for people with disabilities. He observed that many managers who espouse an open-door policy (telling staff that they are always welcome to come in for a chat) often end up conveying, in a thousand small ways, that they are really too busy to be welcoming. "The door of my office may be open, but the door of my heart is closed."[1]

AU   Kindness doesn't come naturally, especially to people who are goal-oriented and fixated on output.

PS   But with the Spirit's empowerment, we can learn the art of putting people at ease and rejoicing in their gifts and achievements.

Rethinking Kindness

We commonly think of kindness in the workplace as being kind to coworkers, to the community, and to oneself. Kindness is caring and respecting colleagues: sharing a cup of coffee, baking cookies for the secretarial pool, chatting with the office cleaner, or helping a new hire feel at ease. Kindness can also be expressed to the wider community: giving spare change to the homeless guy on our way to work, organizing collection boxes for victims of natural disasters, and mobilizing coworkers to help out in a charity. Not least, there's kindness to oneself, which includes managing stress, exercising, and seeking work-life balance. Hard-boiled companies and managers usually dismiss kindness as a fluffy concept that has no impact on the bottom line. But most human resources professionals argue otherwise, asserting that a kind workplace increases employee retention and engagement.

The New Testament Greek word for kindness, *chrēstotēs*, is often associated with God. God reveals kindness by holding back judgment, being willing to forgive, and caring for creation and people by making sun and rain to fall on the just and unjust. God is the ultimate host who created space and time in which we can experience a profound welcome, acceptance, and freedom. In the Psalms, God shows kindness and concern for the poor and afflicted (Ps. 140:12). Above all, God's supreme act of kindness, asserts William Barclay, was demonstrated when Jesus renounced heavenly privileges to take on our lowly human form.[2]

Kindness defuses fear, hidden agendas, and manipulation. It heals conflict. Kindness, says classic commentator Alfred Plummer, is "the sympathetic sweetness of temper which puts others at their ease, and shrinks from giving pain."[3] Kindness stands in diametric opposition to envy. Envy causes us to feel terrible when someone else is happy; kindness causes us to rejoice at the achievements of others. Envy seeks to pull people down; kindness builds people up. In choosing to demonstrate Jesus' kindness, we are choosing the journey toward selflessness.

Kindness at Work

The workplace offers daily opportunities to be aware of God's kindness and to offer that same kindness to people we meet. "Be kind to one another, tender-hearted, as God in Christ has forgiven you," says the apostle Paul (Eph. 4:32). God has forgiven us and showed us compassion. In the same way, we are called to show compassion to unreasonable bosses, to resist the temptation to brush off difficult customers, and to forgive colleagues who wrong us.

Kindness, however, should not be expressed only in one to-one relationships; kindness has to be embodied in the culture and values of the organization. We have a role to play in this. Many modern companies do not embody kindness to staff, especially in their systems, structures, and policies. In an era of downsizing and global competition, shareholders often reward senior management for combining roles and creating greater responsibilities for staff in order to increase productivity and to beat the competition. As a result, people become stressed, overworked, and underpaid.

There's a huge need for people to step forward in embodying the spirit of kindness demonstrated by God. It begins by understanding how organizational culture works. Edgar Schein's seminal study defines the following as key elements of an organization's culture:

1. The observed behavioral regularities in a group (For example, Jill is held up as a model employee for showing up for work fifteen minutes early.)
2. The dominant values of the group (Joe the sales manager implies that any kind of misrepresentation is permissible as long as the deal is clinched.)
3. The rules or "ropes" of the group (John plays squash every week with the boss because it's the way to climb the corporate ladder.)
4. The feeling or climate that is conveyed (Jean has learned to hold back on sharing her concerns during meetings because her colleagues do not welcome negativity.)

Schein says that members of the organization who share the culture and beliefs often do it unconsciously.[4] In most organizations, culture is not formed overnight but through a long process. The charisma of the founder or founders plays a large role in embedding the cultural DNA that determines most of what the company will become. As the company evolves, several things happen:

- Members take on the founder's assumptions, usually subconsciously
- Some companies never "allow" their founder to die or leave, no matter how many successors have come and gone
- Cultures incarnate not only the strengths of founders but also their weaknesses.

It is extremely difficult to transform the culture of a company; many books about change management have been written to address this. Usually, whoever tries to make changes will encounter overt and covert resistance from the culture. Schein suggests that, rather than trying to root out those weaknesses, taking the opposite approach is usually more fruitful: to find out everything we can about the contribution our predecessors have made and to celebrate what they have done for the organization.[5] This allows the members of the organization to move on with new changes.

Cultivating the Fruit of Kindness

Practicing kindness comes more naturally to some people than to others. No matter who we are, the Spirit of God has demonstrated kindness to us through Jesus Christ. So, in our prayers, we can ask God to reveal to us how to show godly kindness toward ourselves and coworkers. Inevitably, we'll discover how we can play a role alongside God in loving diverse people in diverse situations.

Cultivating the Spirit's fruit of kindness could possibly involve:

- Changing attitudes: "I will not wait for others to be kind toward me"; "I will take the first step"; "I will look people in the eye, listen to them attentively, and be sensitive to their unspoken needs."
- Reaching out to subordinates: mentor someone younger who's interested in your career; welcome new hires by treating them to lunch and sharing your "lessons learned"; help someone shy feel at ease; teach a skill and learn from others.
- Reaching out to peers and superiors: listen with compassion; leave a tasty treat or encouraging note for someone you can't get along with or someone who's going through a difficult time; help out overworked colleagues; express appreciation to bosses and supervisors.
- Reaching out to people outside the organization: send thank-you notes to clients and colleagues; mobilize friends and co-workers to donate time and skills to worthy causes; cut down on excessive work hours to spend more time with loved ones.

Exercises

1. Does the culture of your organization embody kindness? How did that come about?

2. In what ways can you contribute to the workplace culture in your sphere of influence (large or small)? What acts of kindness can you practice through changing attitudes, reaching out to people within the organization, and reaching out to stakeholders outside the company?

17

Patience: Remaining Where You Are with Hope

Struggle	Fruit	Outcome
Restlessness Thinking and feeling that there's always something better somewhere else	Patience Having the ability to remain where you are with meaningfulness and hope	Vocational Confidence Experiencing the certainty that you are in God's will and doing God's work

AU   Thank you for challenging me to consider the dangers of restlessness. Rather than running away, it's important to stick it out when things get tough. In light of this, what does it take to work with patience and hope in all that we do?

PS   Frankly, like you, I get restless. Except for the last twenty years where I taught at Regent College, I have moved from assignment to assignment on a regular four-year cycle: pastoring, student counseling, carpentering, doing business, being a dean, teaching, and being a marketplace mentor.

AU   Nevertheless, you've remained in one place, Regent, for a long time. I'm sure you must have learned a thing or two about patience.

PS   Hopefully so. I think of a beautiful word, "longanimity," a fifteenth-century word reintroduced by Cardinal Wyszyński. Longanimity is the ability to go the long haul, choosing not to change things for fairly trivial reasons, and not always longing for new work. This perspective on patience has helped me live out my vocation as a teacher and equipper at Regent College.

Rethinking Patience

The workplace offers a myriad of ways to test our patience: snarled traffic, staff who are slow on the take, pompous bosses, tedious work, irritable colleagues. Small wonder that Margaret Thatcher, Britain's famously short-fused ex-prime minister, was once heard saying: "I am extraordinarily patient, provided I get my own way in the end."

Some people think that patience is a passive posture of helplessness adopted by the weak-spirited. In the Bible, however, the Hebrew and Greek words for "patience" are used to describe God patiently working mighty deeds. God abounds in steadfast love and patience by bearing the sins of people, refusing the rebellion of human beings, and never giving up on people. Jesus is our exemplar. As Lord of lords he patiently bore his human limitations; he was punished for transgressions that were not his own. Jesus' ultimate act of patience lay in choosing to remain on the cross, when he could have ordered heaven's army to rescue him from suffering. That is the character of divine patience.

As a fruit of the Spirit, patience is the work of Jesus Christ, who helps us become more like God by sticking with things, who holds out hope for us and helps us persist in our callings. Above all, patience enables us to fulfill our life's goal of abiding, or remaining, in Jesus Christ. In contrast to restlessness, patience is the ability to remain where we are and to find meaning and hope there.

Therefore we are called to run with "patience" the race marked out for us (Heb. 12:1, KJV) in the same way that Abraham, Job, the Old Testament prophets, Simeon, Paul, John, and the New Testament apostles exercised patience and endured suffering in waiting for God (Heb. 6:15; Job 1:21; James 5:10; Luke 2:25; 2 Tim. 3:10; Rev. 1:9). Evelyn Underhill, a modern Christian mystic, once said that God works in tranquility. And tranquility seldom goes into partnership with speed.[1] Like the other gifts of the Spirit, patience is not something we work up by sheer willpower but by trusting in God in all circumstances.

Patience at Work

We need the Spirit's gift of patience whenever we feel like running away from intractable issues at work. Patience is our greatest ally when we have made a dreadful mistake. Or when we dreamily idolize greener pastures. Or when we've simply run out of courage or motivation.

"The prime virtue gained through daily work is patience," said Cardinal Wyszyński, mentor to the late Pope John Paul II. He likened patience to the rungs of a ladder which, when we climb it, brings us closer to God. That which brings us down that ladder would be the three temptations of longing for new work, being unfaithful in work that has been entrusted to us, and desiring to change jobs for trivial reasons.[2]

If we find ourselves struggling with these temptations, we are most likely wrestling with the question of whether our work is part of our calling. If this particular work is part of our God-given calling, then we should persist. Eighteenth-century Puritan thinker William Perkins developed this thought most eloquently by asserting that everyone is called, and that all callings are equal (whether one is homemaker, pastor, or magistrate). Anyone who becomes a Christian should be assisted to discover his or her calling.[3]

As we seek to be faithful to our calling, we must also be aware of sinful tendencies that erode our ability to persist, such as ambition and envy of other people's callings. The most serious threat undermining our ability to persist in our calling is impatience, which makes us leave our calling when trouble comes. For people tempted to abandon their calling, Perkins, who lived in an era before anesthesia was invented, called for courageous tenacity: "Continue in your calling as a surgeon continues to cut his patient even though the patient screameth much!"[4]

Being patient, however, doesn't mean being inflexible or slow to act. During certain seasons in life, it's necessary to flex and change. Jesus and the apostle Paul showed great adaptability in sharing the gospel and responding to people's needs. However, the general pattern of Jesus' life was to remain true and faithful to his calling. He spent three years walking with his disciples; he had important things to do, but he did not rush.

Cultivating Patience at Work

There are no shortcuts or easy ways to cultivate the Spirit fruit of patience. We may be tempted to try to run faster and to short-circuit the journey toward character transformation. Patience takes time. Often it requires that we remain where we are as we wait for God to move. But what can we do while we wait? We suggest the following:

- *Make it your standard practice to not easily leave whatever you are doing.* When asked by a young disciple about how to please God, Antony of Egypt, the venerable founder of Eastern monasticism, said: "Whoever you may be, always have God before your eyes in whatever you do; do it according to the testimony of the holy Scriptures; *in whatever place you live, do not easily leave it.*"5 This pithy advice applies to almost every occupation. If we stick with things when trouble comes, we will inevitably grow stronger.
- *Reflect on the specific situations that test your patience.* Ambition and envy inhibit patience. You can easily feel restless when you compare yourself to other people who seem to have better jobs and brighter prospects. But before God, you can begin to realize that the very thing that is in your hand — be it your job or project or current responsibility — has great potential for good.

We learn patience not by grinning, grimacing, and bearing pain. To be patient (that is, to remain where we are with meaningfulness and hope) is simply to wait for God's timing. The psalmist declares: "Be still before the LORD and wait patiently for him; do not fret over those who prosper in their ways, over those who carry out evil devices. Refrain from anger, and forsake wrath. Do not fret — it leads only to evil. For the wicked shall be cut off, but those who wait for the LORD will inherit the land" (Ps. 37:7-9). As we wait and hope in God, we are given a new vision of God working in our lives, blessing us with meaning and purpose, empowering us to keep going.

Exercises

1. Identify a specific occasion in the past or present when you felt restless or afflicted by the urge to run away:
   - Did you ask "why me?"
   - Did you feel self-pity?
   - Are you willing to turn to God with a concrete request for renewal in this area?
2. If you are willing to turn to God, you may wish to proceed with the following:
   - In your prayer, affirm that your struggle with restlessness has been decisively defeated by the death and resurrection of Jesus Christ.
   - Breathe in the Spirit's empowering presence, asking God to renew you with the gift of patience.

18

Peace: Bringing Wholeness and Harmony

Struggle	Fruit	Outcome
Boredom Having insufficient passion or interest to give yourself heartily to work and life	Peace Having a passion for completeness and harmony, no matter what the situation	Heavenly-Mindedness Experiencing the meaning and joy of work that will last in view of eternity

AU During our recent canoeing trip together, I sat in a folding chair and watched the sun set behind a heavy bank of clouds that shrouded the mountains in deep purple. I listened to the gentle lapping of the waves against the lakeshore. I wasn't doing anything else, but I wasn't bored. I felt absolute bliss and serenity. Could it be possible that we're created to live in utter calm and peace?

PS You must have forgotten how hard it was for us to paddle the canoe against the wind to get to the lakeside campground.

AU That's true. Achieving a state of bliss was hard work. My arms and back ached for a week after the trip.

PS The peace that God gives us is not about striving for utter calm. It's also not about the absence of stress and pressure. It's about presence — discovering that God is present among us, helping us each step of the way, no matter how crazy things get.

AU I hope I discover God's peace when I return to the world of office politics and back-to-back meetings.

Rethinking Peace

Few people consider the workplace as a sanctuary of peace. Modern companies are beset by cutthroat competition, economic uncertainties, and shareholder concerns. High-performing workers face more pressure to attain even more as they are "rewarded" with increasingly challenging assignments. Laggards are told they need to shape up or ship out. Today, more and more people work under high stress, sacrificing relationships, rest, and reflection along the way. Small wonder that people long for peace — or less stress.

From a Christian perspective, God's peace calls for much more than personal stress management. The peace given to us by Jesus is not about the absence of tension and problems but about presence, says Eugene Peterson, professor emeritus of spiritual theology at Regent College. "There is nothing lethargic or static about peace; it involves total participation in life at its most vital. . . . When we receive God's peace, our experience is not of being removed from conflict so that we can live a quiet, undisturbed life on our own terms. No, we are plunged into life on God's terms, the light-filled action of Father, Son, and Holy Spirit in the three-ring circus of salvation."[1] God's peace is vibrant, passionate, fully alive. It stands in stark contrast to boredom, which sucks the life out of us, sickening us, causing us to lack passion in our work and relationships.

The Hebrew word for peace, *shalom*, means "may you be well." The peace of Christ ushers in right relationships in every sphere of life — with one's self and with colleagues, institutions, and God. Jesus did not come to bring outward calm while storms seethed within communities and corporations. Rather than false peace, he brought a sword that divided truth from falsehood, idolatry from true service of God (Matt. 10:34). Then Jesus took the ultimate step of becoming a "peace offering," placing himself between a righteous God and sinful humanity — atoning for sin and reconciling the two warring parties.

Peace at Work

We can be recipients of God's peace while we work. We can also be channels of God's peace in the workplace. Through at least three different dimensions, we can give and receive God's peace:

1. *Seek peace through righteousness and justice.* True peace requires a passion for completeness and harmony, waging war against evil and injustice, whenever necessary. "Righteousness and peace will kiss each other," declares the psalmist (85:10). Seeking righteousness and justice in the workplace calls us to be attentive to the downtrodden and suffering among us. While it is all too easy to ignore the plight of the needy as we pursue a stress-free life, this would not be true Christian peace.

2. *Seek peace among enemies and those who persecute us.* The peace of Christ is attained by harmonizing diverse people and personalities. We do not arrive at peace by forcing conformity, ignoring tension, or papering over disagreements. "For Jesus," says award-winning author Frederick Buechner, "peace seems to have meant not the absence of struggle but the presence of love."[2]

   Repeatedly, Jesus promises us his peace, not a generic peace, but one that transcends human understanding. "Peace I leave with you; *my* peace I give you," he tells his disciples (John 14:27) shortly before he is arrested, tortured by soldiers, tried by a kangaroo court, ridiculed by religious leaders, and dismissed as a charlatan by passersby. Yet while dying on the cross he forgave everyone — a cosmic act that mystified human understanding but brought harmony to human strife. We have now been blessed with that same peace. When we are betrayed or berated by bosses or colleagues — and we forgive them — surely we are passing the peace of Christ.

The workplace provides numerous opportunities for Christians to grow as peacemakers. Workplace conflict often flares up from small incidents, such as a carelessly worded e-mail or lunchtime gossip. Sometimes, keeping peace means keeping silence. In other situations, Christians must seize opportunities to resolve conflicts by stepping in as mediators. "Peace is right relationships in every sphere of life," says Bible scholar William Barclay.[3]

3. *Seek peace among believers.* Jesus urges us not only to pass the peace to our enemies but also to be at peace with one another (Mark 9:50). However, seeking peace among believers can often be a greater challenge because of our "Christian" tendency to avoid conflict or be nice to one another. Insidious patterns of denial, passive-aggressive indirectness, and unspoken resentments can often be toxic, especially in Christian ministry. By not talking together, we do not work together. The irony, of course, is that most relationships are strengthened as people work through conflict and resolve their differences in a meaningful manner. This requires listening without passing judgment or jumping to conclusions, taking risks, and developing creative options. The default option — pretending that everything's okay — may appear peaceable, but this is false peace. Jerome, the fourth-century doctor of the church, bluntly observed that "as long as we are unable to make peace with our brother, I do not know whether we may offer our gifts to God."[4]

Cultivating the Fruit of Peace

Jesus was comfortable with himself, whether in groups or alone. He was not flustered by crowds but welcomed them. He valued solitude but did not become a recluse. Caught in a storm that terrified experienced fishermen, Jesus remained calm. Jesus, the human embodiment of God, maintained his equilibrium amid the complexity of life. Sought out as a wise counselor, but then ridiculed and mobbed, and then rejected by people, he rested in the knowledge that even the worst, if it happens, will be for the best. That inner certainty is peace.

We, too, can receive this peace that Christ embodies. Fundamentally, we must acknowledge that we are enemies of God due to the evil in our hearts. But thanks to the Lord Jesus Christ, we have become friends of God and therefore enemies of evil. Origen, the great second-century theologian, observed that "we shall have even greater peace with God if we continue our active hostility toward the devil and fight against the vices of the flesh."[5] This new relationship far surpasses the Greeks' ancient search for *ataraxia* (tranquility, quiet mind, total indifference, stillness). As we wage war against evil and desire peace with God, the God of peace reveals himself.

Exercise

Read Philippians 4:6-9 and invite the God of peace to enter your life's circumstances, especially the workplace. You may wish to practice the following:

- Do not worry (a sin that undermines our trust in God). "Do not be anxious about anything," says Paul. The decision to trust — and not worry — requires daily vigilance. As you work, become more attentive to any worrisome thoughts that trouble you during the day.
- Pray. Rather than become obsessed about your worries, name these worrisome thoughts and share them with God (1 Pet. 5:7). The workplace provides ample opportunity for practicing this! Also take time to specify moments of gratitude (Phil. 4:6).
- Think on holy things. In your daily work, articulate the small but significant moments that are noble, right, pure, lovely, admirable, excellent, and praiseworthy. We recommend that you do this after dinner or before bed. You'll be surprised how every day will yield a harvest of praiseworthy things (Phil. 4:7).

PART THREE

Nine Fruits of Workplace Spirituality

Outcomes of a Spirit-Led Life

As we experience freedom from the soul-sapping struggles and our lives become more infused with the Spirit's work, our attitude toward work will change.

We will begin to work prayerfully and consider work to be living prayer. The quality of our work will be characterized by gratitude and purity of motivation. Though we might win praise and financial gain for our work, we understand the need for ongoing relinquishment and surrendered contentment. Instead of seeking work-life balance, our life will be governed by a life-giving rhythm and spurred by love of neighbor. Not least, we will gain an unshakable confidence in our God-given vocation; we know that at least some of our work will not be in vain, but will endure in the new heaven and new earth.

The nine outcomes below — which describe results of the Spirit's work in our lives — are by no means exhaustive. There is much more to experience besides the nine outcomes we've identified. This is only the beginning.

The Spirit's work in our lives is gradual and good. We *will* be changed for the better. But does that also mean that we will always find increasing satisfaction in our daily work?

This question preoccupied Qoheleth, the Hebrew professor of philosophy who wrote the book of Ecclesiastes. He asked, "What do mortals get from all the toil and strain with which they toil under the sun?" (Eccles. 2:22). Qoheleth responded to his own

Struggles	Fruit	Outcomes
Pride	Joy	Continuous Prayer
Greed	Goodness	Persistent Gratitude
Lust	Love	Beautiful Purity
Gluttony	Self-Control	Joyful Relinquishment
Anger	Gentleness	Surrendered Contentment
Sloth	Faithfulness	Life-Giving Rhythms
Envy	Kindness	Neighbor-Love
Restlessness	Patience	Vocational Confidence
Boredom	Peace	Heavenly-Mindedness

question with a profound insight: We will not find life's deepest satisfaction in doing the work itself, but we find deepest satisfaction in being with God, who works alongside us.

Many of us say we want to work *for* God. Indeed, we have encountered pastors, missionaries, accountants, business executives, and homemakers whose sincere and heartfelt goal is to work for God. But the apostle Paul, himself a tentmaker and disciple-maker, hinted on the ominous possibility that such work could be in vain (see 1 Cor. 15:58). The key thing that safeguards our work from becoming futile, meaningless, and worthless is that we perform the work in faith, hope, and love for Jesus Christ (1 Thess. 1:3).

In this way, work is like an evangelist that draws us closer to Jesus Christ, if we have the right motivations and attitude. Jesus does not promise us the good news that we will be supremely happy and successful in our jobs. Jesus promises us better news: In our work, we will find satisfaction in him. He alone can fill the God-shaped vacuum in our souls.

In hiddenness and humility, Jesus comes to us in the workplace not to dictate what we should do with our lives but to offer himself as our companion on the journey.

19

Continuous Prayer

Struggle	Fruit	Outcome
Pride Being imprisoned within your self as No. 1	Joy Feeling the exhilaration of having God as No. 1	Continuous Prayer Experiencing continuous communion with God

AU Some days, during unexpected moments at work, I'm surprised by joy. It's an awareness of God's abiding presence — I'm working with God, and my work matters to God.

PS Have you always had these experiences of God's presence with you in the workplace?

AU Absolutely not. I've never considered myself to be a prayerful person to begin with. However, when I pursued theological studies during my sabbatical, I read about ancient Christians who aspired to "pray *without ceasing*" and to "give thanks in *all* circumstances" (1 Thess. 5:17-18). It sounded impossible that anyone could pray all the time. But I tried to put it into practice as I wrote theological papers. I prayed before I began an assignment. Writing prayerfully, without anxiety or rush, I would thank God for the insights. Each keystroke would be an act of worship. When the work was done, I thanked God for helping me. Slowly I began to see that my work — and the process of working — could be a form of prayer. God was helping me become more aware of God's movements in my heart.

PS What was it like when you got a "real" job again?

AU At first, I felt as if my world had caved in. I was stressed and often paralyzed by deadlines, and I couldn't pray. And I was too worried to think about God. One day, however, I was struck by a simple thought: I should regard my workplace as a "monastery" where God is already present. I could pray quick, short prayers for my colleagues during work. During lunch, I imagined Jesus Christ as our unseen conversation partner. When I felt stuck, I would ask God for help. So there were lots of opportunities to pray, because I felt stuck so many times a day! Slowly, I realized that God had been keeping company with me all this while — even when I did not naturally turn to God.

PS Your story reminds me of many of God's people in the Bible: Abraham, Moses, David, Boaz, Ruth, Nehemiah, Daniel, Jesus, and Paul. When we consider the variety of work they did — prophet, nation-builder, shepherd, administrator, judge, warrior, king, poet, gleaner, homemaker, just to mention a few — we see that their kind of work was not very conducive to prayer. Yet they prayed before work, during work, and after work. They experienced communion and friendship with God.

AU And they prayed in so many different ways while they worked. They prayed with words. They prayed in silence. They sang and shouted, they moaned and groaned. They shared their joy, anger, despair, thanksgiving, and frustrations with God. They prayed with their friends and colleagues. But they also prayed in private, when no one was watching.

Work and Prayer

Without prayer our work life is impoverished. The apostle Paul demonstrated the richness of joining prayer and work. Besides writing about prayer, he prayed as he wrote the letters that were a part of his pastoral work. For example, when Paul writes to Christians in Colossae, prayer and work frame the beginning and ending of his letter about what the new life in Christ looks like (Col. 1:3, 9-12). For Paul, there's no clear separation between prayer and work:

- Prayer and work are directed to God (Col. 1:3, 9, 12; 3:23).
- Both are animated and energized by Jesus Christ (1:11, 29).
- We work and pray with wholeheartedness and joy (3:23; 4:2).
- Prayer and work require continued attention (1:3, 9).
- Prayer leads us toward a life of good work and carrying out Christ's work (1:9, 10; 3:3, 4), while work leads us toward depending on Christ's power through prayer (1:29).
- Work strengthens our relationship with the Father (3:23), while prayer makes us thankful to the Father (1:12).

Taken together, prayer and work are synergistic. "It is not possible to do lasting, versatile, fruitful, and effective work without linking it with prayer," says Cardinal Wyszyński.[1] When we work prayerfully we will:

- See people through God's eyes and be able to speak the truth, comfort the hurting, help the hopeless, and listen to the lonely.
- Become aware that God is guiding us even in the most frustrating experiences at work.
- Find ourselves overcoming pride.
- Discover joy in the work that we do.
- Be inundated with hope that the products of our minds and hands — no matter how menial — will have eternal value.

A minister once asked the Indian mystic Sadhu Sundar Singh, "Do we need to pray more, or to work more, or to divide our time in doing both?" Singh replied: "Both are equally necessary. Prayer without work is as bad as work without prayer. As a clucking hen to satisfy its instinct continues to sit in some dark corner even after its eggs have been removed, so the life of those who remove themselves from the busy life of the world and spend their time wholly in prayer is as fruitless as is the hen's."[2]

An Example: The Prayerful Chef

Nicolas Herman, commonly known as Brother Lawrence, became a cook in a Carmelite monastery in Paris in 1666. Because he was not an ordained monk, he did not pray upstairs with the clergy and ordained monks. Instead, he worshiped God amid the clatter of pots and pans in the hot kitchen. As the years passed, the monks and people outside his monastery felt that Brother Lawrence had somehow discovered an amazing sense of the presence of God in his life. They peppered him with questions and letters on how to be aware of God while working. Brother Lawrence's conversations and written replies were eventually compiled into *The Practice of the Presence of God.*

Consider a few of Brother Lawrence's observations, which we have adapted for readability. They shed wonderful insights on what it means to be praying continuously while working:

- In order to form a habit of conversing with God continually and referring all we do to him, we must first attend to him with some diligence. After some attentive care, we should find his love inwardly exciting us to it without any difficulty.
- When we are offered an occasion to practice some virtuous act, we must address ourselves to God, saying, Lord, I cannot do this unless you enable me. When we do this, we receive strength more than sufficient.[3]
- When I failed in my duty, I confessed to God, saying, I shall never do otherwise if you leave me to myself; it is you who must hinder my falling and mend what is amiss. After this, I gave myself no further uneasiness about it.[4]
- For me the set times of prayer are not different from other times. I retire to pray, according to the directions of my superiors, but I do not want such retirement, nor ask for it, because my greatest business does not divert me from God.

- When I fail in my duty, I readily acknowledge it, saying, I am used to failing; I shall never do otherwise if I am left to myself. If I do not fail, then I give God thanks, acknowledging that the strength comes from him.[5]

Exercise

Which of Brother Lawrence's prayers is appropriate for you to put into practice today in your workplace?

20

Persistent Gratitude

Struggle	Fruit	Outcome
Greed Inflaming the passion to possess more than you have	Goodness Cultivating a character that gives rather than takes	Persistent Gratitude Experiencing the freedom of knowing that all you have comes from God

AU   I've met senior executives who don't feel grateful for their work or haven't found time to enjoy what they already have. If it seems so hard for wealthy and accomplished people to feel gratefulness, what about the rest of us?

PS   Ever since I was young, I've been fortunate to meet grateful people. And they usually were counted among the poor. My grandfather, for example, was a fisherman who sailed his schooner to Labrador to fish for six months of the year. He had no auxiliary engine or radar. But every day, he always expressed thanks for the fish he caught and for safe travel.

AU   Have you ever been poor yourself?

PS   There have also been seasons in my life when I didn't have much. My wife Gail and I lived in the inner city of Montreal for six years, experiencing poverty as we worked alongside the poor. I've also worked as a tradesperson for six years. Through it all, I have learned that it is not the amount of money we make, the prestige of the job, or the social importance of the work that makes us greedy or thankful. Instead, it is the predisposition of our soul. A heart of gratitude lies in being content with what we have and recognizing that everything that comes our way — including trials and setbacks — is a gift.

AU Gratitude also delivers us from a lot of workplace struggles. When you're grateful, you don't think of quitting for the wrong reasons. You do not envy someone else's job. Gratefulness kills a grumbling and complaining spirit. You can't be angry and grateful at the same time. Gratitude really does safeguard us from falling into sin.

Work and Gratitude

We depend on God for everything: provision, protection, joy, work, relationships, family, and ultimately life itself. Therefore, being grateful lies at the heart of what it means to be a human being. It is inhuman to be ungrateful.

The journey from greed to goodness requires that we recognize that we are not autonomous. Orthodox theologian Alexander Schmemann notes how fundamentally our sin is rooted in our lack of gratitude (or *eucharist,* the Greek word for thanksgiving): "In the biblical story of creation, man is presented as a hungry being, and the whole world his food. . . . The 'original' sin is not primarily that man has disobeyed God; the sin is that he ceased to be hungry for him and for him alone. The only real fall of man is his noneucharistic life in a noneucharistic world."[1]

We pile disaster upon ourselves when we refuse to revere or give thanks to God, says the apostle Paul. In the first chapter of Romans, Paul describes a catalog of sins — sexual confusion, gossip, idolatry, and murder — and notes that all these stem from the primal sin: irreverence and ingratitude. The heart of sin lies in our willful refusal to thank God even though we know all along that there is a God.

The exact opposite happens when we express gratitude to

God. Gratitude is the truest response to who God is and who we are. And one of the outcomes of being filled by God's Spirit is that we lead grateful lives. What does a grateful life look like?

1. *A grateful life transforms how we view and experience work.* When we are thankful for everything, we discover that problems, difficult colleagues, and personal struggles and losses become means of grace and learning. Gratitude opens up new pathways to growth in Christ-like character. It is in walking through life's crucibles — as Jesus did on his journey toward the cross — that we become like Jesus and experience God-with-us. Along the way, gratitude transforms our relationships with coworkers into mutual, two-way transactions. "When gratitude is the source of our actions, our giving becomes receiving and those to whom we minister become our ministers," says author Henri Nouwen.[2] Thanksgiving sanctifies life.

2. *Persistent gratitude releases us from being controlled by how good or bad things are.* Through gratitude we gain a God-sized view of life. At its most basic, thanksgiving delivers us from discontentment. Gradually we gain clearer insight into what God is doing in our lives and workplace — things are not merely as they seem. A life of prolonged gratitude — thanking God in seasons of both plenty and famine — is simply a childlike trust that God is God and we are not.

3. *Thanksgiving gives God God's due.* Daily work is full of situations where even an occasional breathed word of thanksgiving can be transformative. For which of these do you wish to say thanks to God today?
   - Your co-workers
   - Your boss or supervisor or anyone else to whom you are held accountable
   - The corporation or organization where you are employed or work as a volunteer
   - A performance review
   - Hard experiences when you are confronted with your own inadequacies
   - A challenge or seemingly insoluble problem

- A failed project
- A successful project
- A bright idea that will improve systems and processes
- A breakthrough in a production, service, or marketing challenge
- Financial concerns
- Provision and pay
- A cup of coffee or drink enjoyed during a break
- A lunch conversation
- The very fact that you are able to work
- The work that you have been given to do

An Example: The Grateful Dentist

After becoming a Christian in university, David Gunaratnam wanted to become a missionary. However, when he earned his degree in dentistry, he felt called to pattern his life after the apostle Paul, who worked as a tentmaker while ministering to God's people. For David, this meant joining the civil service as a dentist and working in small towns in rural Malaysia. He developed his dental practice with faithfulness, quietly gaining renown for his skillful hands and gentle demeanor. He later received one of the country's highest honorific titles for his services.

And yet there is much more to David than his vocational identity. His biggest legacy is the lives of Christians David discipled and shaped over the past five decades — many of whom are now senior pastors, theologians, missionaries, and leaders of organizations in Malaysia and throughout the world. As one, they describe "David G." as a man who is humble, discerning, and profoundly grateful toward God.

David's gratitude is all the more remarkable because he and his wife Christina have two children, one of whom has severe autism. Mark, who is now thirty-three years old, has the aptitude of a three-year-old child. In appearance a fine young man, Mark requires intense care-giving; he cannot be left alone.

"When Mark was diagnosed as severely autistic with an IQ of

60, Christina and I were in shock," David said. But while reading the book of Job, David was struck by an epiphany: in times of suffering, it is better to ask for God's self-revelation than to ask why God allows the righteous to suffer. "We felt led to walk through the pain and to pray, 'Lord, just show us yourself.' And in the goodness of the Lord, we were overwhelmed by God's presence with us — even as we allowed the Lord to take control of our lives."

And what has loving Mark taught David and Christina about gratefulness?

First, they discovered that God has given them genuine love for Mark. During the early years they knew they'd be unable to generate the gentle love needed to care for their son — not while Mark was tearing apart books, writing on the walls, and ripping up furniture. "It's a love that comes from God," David said.

Second, David and Christina found that their relationship has grown deeper. At times, they felt at wit's end in helping one another with caring for Mark. But through prayer, they came to understand that Christina's main ministry would be to serve Mark, while David's ministry would be to serve his wife. The challenges of caring for their son created a genuine bond with their son — and between them.

Third, they discovered freedom to minister to people in a radical new way, with God at the center. The severe curtailment of their personal freedom — because Mark needed constant care and supervision — meant that their home could have felt like prison. Instead, it became a hospitable space for neighbors, church members, friends, strangers, patients, and even David's nursing staff, all of whom were drawn to their living room for Bible studies, counseling sessions, and conversations. They've all met Mark, of course. "God has revolutionized our thinking and approach to Christian ministry because of Mark. We realized that for the Lord to accomplish his will, Mark must be a part of the family," David said.

People who've visited their home say they've been profoundly changed because of observing this family, as well as being blessed by David's gift for mentoring people and being an attentive listener.

"The difficult circumstances that David G. has faced in raising Mark add weight to his wisdom," said David Tan, a lay leader of a local church. "When you talk to him, he's thankful and grateful that you know him and that he knows you. He listens very intently to you, hanging on to every word, because everything you say is important. He makes sure he understands you perfectly. You get the sense that he's *truly grateful* because he has met you. What a rare quality to find in a person."

Exercise

What are you truly grateful for in this season of your work life?

21

Beautiful Purity

Struggle	Fruit	Outcome
Lust Imagining how people can be used for self-interest	Love Practically caring for the best interests of others	Beautiful Purity Experiencing whole-hearted love for God and neighbor

AU I've seen lots of people, including me, who work in a half-hearted manner. Or people might work hard solely because they want to get ahead. But it's less common to see a person who works wholeheartedly out of good and pure motivations. Paul, what does it look like for us to work with purity of heart?

PS The Bible states that the pure in heart shall see God in all spheres of life — including the workplace. Our hearts become deeply aligned with God's heart. And we truly love our neighbors, including our colleagues, as ourselves.

AU If that's the case, I've fallen far short of the mark. And I could do much more in caring for the best interests of others.

PS The experience of a pure heart is not reserved for the sinless. Sinners deeply pained by their frailties and weaknesses have the greatest potential to experience purity of heart. Purity of heart is for those who stumble, fumble, and fall. It is also for those of us who are filled with joy when we discover that we're working with a pure motivation of love. Like King David, we beseech God, "Create in me a clean heart."

Work and Purity

Purity is beautiful. But it is not beautiful to those who resist God. How do we gain purity? While only God can create a pure heart (Ps. 51:12; Prov. 29:9), the journey toward purity of heart requires active struggle on our part to subdue sin (Ps. 73:13-14).

When we work with purity of heart, we will:

1. *See God in all spheres of life — including the workplace (Ps. 24:3-4).* Biblical writers suggest that a pure heart is empty, ready to be filled by God's love and commandments, while the hearts of the wicked are stuffed with thoughts of well-being, wealth, pride, and malice (see Pss. 41:7 and 73:7). As we walk with God and work wholeheartedly, we become upright and blameless people (Ps. 119:80). We gain the eyes to see God renewing and redeeming our workplaces. "Blessed are the pure in heart, for they will see God," said Jesus (Matt. 5:8).

2. *Experience God working through us.* We will work with one aim: to be one with Jesus Christ and to share his goal of working alongside the Father (John 5:19, 36). We will join Jesus in bringing about God's kingdom by caring for every sphere of life: creation, neighborhoods, workplaces, churches, families, the poor and the rich, the healthy and the sick, the weak and the strong.

3. *Will one thing.* We will always say yes to God. In fact, we will do whatever it takes to ensure that nothing gets in the way of our journey toward God. "God is one and all," said the Danish philosopher Søren Kierkegaard, "therefore the pure in heart will one thing."[1] Speaking through the prophet Jeremiah, God promised people "singleness of heart and action" (Jer. 32:39). This theme emerges in the teachings and the lives

of great souls throughout history. In twentieth-century India, Mother Teresa echoed this theme: "Your vocation is to belong to Jesus."[2]

4. *Live an undivided life.* The pure in heart experience coherence of words, thoughts, and deeds: our public and private lives are in sync. We will speak, think, or do the right thing, whether or not anyone is watching us. We will not be driven by inner compulsions or external motivations. Rather, our actions will be motivated by love, joy, and peace that come from the presence and power of the risen Christ working with us and within us in every aspect of our lives.

5. *Be joined to God.* The outcome of purity of heart is to love God for who God is — no more, no less. God is all that we love and all that we want. John Cassian, chronicler of the wisdom of the desert fathers, said that a pure heart is the entryway into the heart of our Trinitarian God: "[God] will be all that we are zealous for, all that we strive for. He will be all that we think about, all our living, all that we talk about, our very breath. And that union of Father and Son, of Son and Father, will fill our senses and our minds."[3]

An Example: A Pure Bureaucrat

Life in the workplace can be hard, hurtful, and downright scary, especially in politics. People may resent you and try to bring you down. Daniel, a young Hebrew man, experienced this firsthand. As a believing Jew, he was exiled to ancient Babylon to be schooled as a bureaucrat in the pagan Babylonian court. Like most civil servants, he worked under several consecutive governments. Gifted with innate intellect, verbal skills, and integrity, Daniel vaulted to the most elite positions in the world's largest empire at that time. Officials envied Daniel's success and tried unsuccessfully to derail his political career. In a long series of twists and turns that led to an elaborate plot to murder Daniel, his purity of heart was revealed in several ways:

- *In a time of crisis, Daniel did not panic; he prayed and glorified God.* At one time, King Nebuchadnezzar was about to execute all the wise men of Babylon because they could not interpret the meaning of his dream. Daniel and his friends prayed, received the interpretation, and told the astonished king what the dream meant. On both occasions when Daniel was called before the king to interpret dreams, Daniel gave credit to God (Dan. 4:1-37).

- *Daniel did not flinch from speaking the truth — no matter how difficult.* Another king, Belshazzar, saw a frightening vision while feasting. The king's wife said to her husband, "There is a man in your kingdom who is endowed with the spirit of the holy gods" (Dan. 5:11). So once again Daniel stood before the king and told the unvarnished truth — that the king's days were numbered because of his spiritual debauchery.

- *Daniel led an utterly blameless life.* In his later years, Daniel was elevated to the third highest position in Babylon. King Darius, Daniel's next boss, also liked Daniel. Envious administrators tried to dig up dirt on Daniel but learned something everyone else already knew: Daniel was unimpeachable. "They could find no . . . corruption [in Daniel], because he was faithful and no negligence or corruption could be found in him" (Dan. 6:4). Because they couldn't expose Daniel for bad behavior, they resolved to attack him for his single-minded pure love and faith in God. (Leading a blameless life does not exempt us from trials and opposition.)

- *Daniel cultivated a vibrant prayer life — no matter the cost.* Daniel's loyalty to God in the moment of crisis was no accident. Forced to choose between not praying daily to his God and being eaten by lions, Daniel chose the latter. He knew the source of his success and guidance for each new day came from God. So no matter how busy or dangerous things became for Daniel, he never neglected prayer. In the lions' den, God rescued Daniel. But even if Daniel had not lived to tell the tale, he had made it evident that his relationship with God mattered more than anything else, even life itself.

Exercise

In what areas of your work-life do you desire to develop consistency of word and action?

22

Joyful Relinquishment

Struggle	Fruit	Outcome
Gluttony Looking for satisfaction through excessive consumption	Self-Control Being governed by godly living and the Spirit's leading	Joyful Relinquishment Experiencing the freedom to release a preoccupation with food and to eat more simply

PS Since our first conversation, do you think you're gradually being transformed by God into a person with self-control? Have you found greater freedom from excessive consumption?

AU My wife and I have been finding creative ways to voluntarily relinquish things. For example, in a middle-class culture where it's normal for a husband and wife to own two cars and two cell phones, we have chosen to share one car and one cell phone. We certainly aren't suffering. It's our small way of saying no to excessive consumption and saying yes to self-control.

PS How did this journey of relinquishment begin for you?

AU One day, while I was reading the Bible, a thought popped into my head: "Stop reading mystery novels." I knew the thought could not have come from me because I loved reading mystery novels. In fact, I used to devour four books a week while working and studying. But I knew that God, in a mysterious way, had spoken to me. So I stopped reading mystery novels. As the weeks passed, I was finally able to admit that I had become obsessed with reading the novels. Reading late into the night was fueling my addictive personality, which became an entryway for other soul-sapping struggles, such as lust, pride, sloth, and restlessness. I discovered that by stopping an indulgent habit, I was able to pray and work with greater joy. And I was no longer such an easily distracted person.

PS Sounds like you've experienced the joy of relinquishment. For most people, relinquishment sounds terribly unappealing. I once saw a cartoon of a man being baptized by immersion. The pastor said that everything that goes under the water belongs to God. The last frame shows the man underwater with his hand above the water still grasping his wallet!

AU The wonderful thing about practicing relinquishment is that it frees us from a grasping spirit. We relinquish the things that have a stronger grip on our soul than God — be it possessions, social standing, family ties, friendships, or bodily needs.

PS Wouldn't it be wonderful for Christians in the workplace to practice relinquishment — especially in the area of money? As we practice relinquishment, we'll experience greater freedom to release possessions to live with greater simplicity, in alignment with God.

Work and Relinquishment

When we work with a deep sense of ongoing relinquishment, we will:

1. *Be content with our wages.* This was exactly what John the Baptist told the soldiers who sought him out for counsel (Luke 3:14). John's advice assumes that the soldiers were being paid fair wages, just as the apostle Paul instructed Christian employers ("masters") in the city of Colossae to pay their servants "justly and fairly" (Col. 4:1). For today's middle-class

workers who enjoy salaries that are benchmarked according to market rates, being content with wages is an indicator that we're on the path toward relinquishment. The practice of relinquishment is an important safeguard from the constant push for more and more — an upward trajectory that can become counter-productive if one becomes "too expensive to retain."

2. *Become free from the idolatry of money.* Money can be a means of grace; it can also be a death-dealing god. Jesus made this plain and clear in his encounter with a wealthy young man (Matt. 19:16-26). The young man had approached Jesus asking: "Teacher, what good deed must I do to have eternal life?" (19:16). Though he was financially successful, the man's poignant question reveals that money never satisfies. He felt an emptiness and longed for something more. Diagnosing the man's deepest ills, Jesus said, "If you wish to be perfect, *go, sell* your possessions and *give* the money to the poor, and you will have treasure in heaven; then come, *follow* me" (19:21). Shackled by the idolatry of money, the man walked away sorrowfully. But those of us who learn the art of ongoing relinquishment will find joy in the ongoing process of going, selling, and giving to the poor. As we do this, we gain the kingdom of God. We gain our eternal treasure: Jesus Christ.

3. *Engage successfully in spiritual warfare against the stranglehold money has over people, organizations, and even the church.* This spiritual warfare is unceasing, even for the greatest saints, because money is not a neutral medium of exchange; money has the ability to inspire devotion. "Those who love money never have enough," declared the philosophical writer of Ecclesiastes (5:10, TNIV). Money makes us covet only the things money can buy.[1] It makes us feel secure, guilty, and beholden to it — money is like a deity. "You cannot serve God and wealth," says Jesus (Luke 16:13). In the midst of a greedy and needy world, the real reason for embracing simplicity and relinquishment is to reflect the values of the kingdom of God.[2]

4. *Experience the joy of giving.* "Gain all you can, save all you can,

give all you can," declared the preacher John Wesley in his sermon on "The Use of Money."[3] Wesley's famous dictum is within reach for us. Jesus may not call everyone to sell all possessions as he did with the rich young man, but we are all called to give generously, as Zacchaeus the tax-collector did the moment he experienced Jesus' friendship.

An Example: A Simpler-Living Business Executive

One afternoon, Barney (not his real name) roared into the parking lot on his motorbike and took off his helmet. "Paul, I was just thinking and praying for you!" he declared.

I found this to be so characteristic of Barney, a gentle and soft-spoken senior executive of a global IT company who was always praying for people in his heart, like a true priest. Many times Barney has telephoned me and said, "This morning God put you on my heart. Is everything okay?" Barney always had the uncanny knack of doing this at a moment of personal need.

When he was part of the senior management team, Barnabas could have lived "high on the hog," but he and his wife Rachel had opted to live more simply by practicing the "theology of enough."[4] Compared to his peers, Barney lived in a modest North Vancouver home, drove a modest vehicle, and enjoyed modest local vacations. Barney and Rachel shared one car. They had enough.

Barney also chose the path of downward mobility. On one occasion, when offered a promotion, he asked instead to be demoted. Barney wasn't afraid of additional wealth or responsibilities. What troubled Barney was that this new job he was being offered would take him away from caring directly for colleagues. This was the very thing he was most gifted in — an integral part of his calling to be a pastor in the marketplace. So he asked for — and got — a demotion. The significant pay cut and lighter workload also gave him significantly more time to spend with his wife, family, and neighbors.

When Barney retired from his executive position, he did not retire from his calling. Continuing on his path of downward mobility, Barney now rides the bus or his motorcycle to save on parking fees. He continues to care for people living downtown, especially the bicycle couriers, who regard him as a chaplain. He volunteers as an escort for prisoners who are temporarily leaving prison to visit their families. He does all these things and more for the sake of Jesus Christ whom he loves.

Exercise

How much is "enough" for you? Think of this in terms of housing, vehicles, vacations, clothing, and eating out.

23

Surrendered Contentment

Struggle	Fruit	Outcome
Anger Using passion to manipu- late and control people and circumstances	Gentleness Empowering others by renouncing personal agendas and expressing meekness	Surrendered Contentment Experiencing the satis- faction of who you are, what you have, and what you do

AU Paul, I think I'm learning to complain less these days. I didn't know that I was a whiner when things got tough. Then one night, while I was eating dinner with my wife and a friend, I heard God's voice telling me to stop complaining.

PS God told you to stop complaining?

AU Yes, I think so. I was telling my dinner companions about my workplace woes: the long hours, the stress, the relentless work, and how I felt ignorant and stupid all the time. On and on I went. Then suddenly, I heard two words: Stop complaining. The voice was gentle but firm. And I was taken aback. Had I been complaining? Immediately, I realized I had been whining for an entire hour! I made a snap decision: I would stop complaining.

PS And what did you discover?

AU That I complained much more than I realized. And it was

very difficult to stop. But I also discovered that I was becoming less fearful, doubtful, and self-pitying. I was walking into the office with a confident stride and a smile. I discovered more and more things to be thankful about every day.

PS The more you complained, the more you gave in to fear. By not complaining, you broke the vicious cycle. You gradually gained the courage to confront situations that troubled you. And it sounds like you became much more contented once you surrendered your complaints to God.

Work and Surrender

How much money do we need before we know it's enough? That was a question that I (Alvin) posed to my friend, who worked with me in Malaysia's largest telecommunications company.

"How much is enough?" I asked John Tan (not his real name).

"Five million," John said.

"Okay," I said. Then I recalled that he already owned several houses in a wealthy suburb. "Sounds like you're almost there."

"No, no, no," he said, with a wave of his hands. "The five million doesn't include stocks, assets, and homes. I'm looking for five more million — cash."

A few years later, John and I met for lunch (his treat). We had both moved on to other jobs. He was now a senior vice president of a startup telecommunications company. I reminded him of our earlier conversation years ago.

"How's the big five coming along?" I asked.

"The goalpost has changed," he said. "Inflation has soared. I need to provide for my children's education. I'm now looking at fifteen."

Most people balk at the notion of living a contented lifestyle. We instinctively feel the need for more and more. It's hard to be satisfied with what we have. However, Christians are called to live a surrendered life. Such a surrendered life need not be a weakness but can be a position of strength. We are imitating the Lord Jesus, who demonstrated inner strength by walking resolutely toward the cross because he had surrendered his will to his loving Father.

This life of ongoing surrender is one of the outcomes of being filled by God's Spirit. When we live in surrender to God, we will:

1. *Stop trying to control everything and everyone.* Anger is the burning desire to control (we do this directly or indirectly when we seethe in silence, gossip, feel frustrated, berate ourselves for our stupidity, or feel irritable). The antidote to anger is an ongoing surrender to a trustworthy God. This does not mean we abdicate responsibility. Rather, we gain the ability to wield authority without being manipulative or controlling.

2. *Accept whatever God gives us in life and work.* Some people feel that God has withheld from them the joy of "fulfilling work." With surrender, frustration with God is transformed into courage to accept whatever God gives and to give whatever God requires, because God has given himself to us. The great spiritual saints could have become angry with God as they faced problems beyond their control such as mockery, diseases, abandonment, and martyrdom. But they accepted whatever God gave them. "Come then . . . let us be resigned to our frailty and dependence on God, who would never reduce us to being unable to walk on our own feet if he had not the mercy to carry us in his arms," writes Jean-Pierre de Caussade, a Jesuit priest who was described by his peers as "a friend of God" even as he struggled with the drudgery of administrative duties and a life of anonymity.[1] Mother Teresa of Calcutta, another exemplar of the surrendered life, said: "I belong to Jesus. He can do to me whatever he wants."[2]

3. *Experience deep contentment.* We know that we are nothing without God; we acknowledge that everything we have belongs to God, including the struggles of life. We are thankful for everything. "To discover God in the smallest and most ordinary things, as well as in the greatest, is to possess a rare and sublime faith. To find contentment in the present moment is to relish and adore the divine will in the succession of all the

things to be done and suffered which make up the duty to the present moment," writes de Caussade.[3]

An Example: The Contented Farm Worker

Set in a time of moral and political chaos in ancient Israel, the book of Ruth tells the story of a Moabite woman who joined her mother-in-law in resettling in Bethlehem, six miles south of Israel's capital, Jerusalem. Ruth faced overwhelming odds in adjusting to life in a new country: the locals were generally hostile toward Moabites; she was a widow with few prospects of remarriage; and not least, Ruth also had to care for Naomi, her widowed, bereft, and embittered mother-in-law. Most people in Ruth's position would have fallen into despair. But Ruth showed resilience by going to a nearby farm and gleaning stray stalks of barley left behind by harvesters. In a serendipitous twist of events, Boaz, the landowner, fell in love with Ruth, they married, and they had a son whose progeny would include King David and Jesus Christ.

While this story ends joyously for Ruth, Boaz, and Naomi, what interests us most is Ruth's radical trust in God as she battled the odds. What helped Ruth make the journey of surrendered contentment?

- *Ruth gave herself completely* — to Naomi and to God. She held nothing back in her radical decision to follow Naomi to Israel: "Where you go, I will go; where you lodge, I will lodge; your people shall be my people, and your God my God. Where you die, I will die — there I will be buried," Ruth said (1:16-17). Ruth renounced any self-chosen plans. She held on to nothing but her newfound trust in God. Similarly, François Fenelon, the seventeenth-century spiritual director, has noted that in the spiritual life, "we must give all . . . when God asks it. If we have not courage to give, at least we can let him take."[4]
- *Ruth lived fully in the present.* Surrendering to God's plans does not mean passivity or a wistful longing for the past. Ruth responded proactively to the opportunities of each day, no

matter how small. Since she and Naomi had arrived in Israel during the barley harvest, she resolved to pick up gleanings from the edge of a field, even though the task seemed futile (1:22–2:2). Ruth's creativity turned evil days into good. "Sometimes what seems evil becomes good if we leave it to God and do not forestall him with our impatience," says Fenelon.[5]

• *Ruth learned to be faithful in small things.* She accepted the toil and hardship of work (Ruth 2:7, 17, 18). Day after day, she worked without resentment or self-pity. She was not fixated on the big things in life. She did not preoccupy herself with trying to marry a rich landowner, or give birth to a child, or become accepted into society. She simply did her job faithfully — and did not despise her lowly work.

• *Ruth embraced the hardships — and the blessings.* Despite her strength and determination, she didn't cling to self-sufficiency or resist being a recipient of mercy and love (2:10-14, 21; 3:17; 4:13-15). In response to Naomi's matchmaking advice, Ruth said, "I'll do whatever you say" (3:5-6). She accepted Boaz's hospitality and generous sharing of food with grateful thanks. Ruth's embrace of both life's pains and joys made her a receptacle of God's loving-kindness.

• *Ruth learned the art of waiting.* Despite Ruth's track record of taking bold initiatives, she was not wracked by anxiety when she had to wait in times of acute uncertainty. For example, after boldly hinting to Boaz of her willingness to be engaged to marry him, Boaz told her to "remain this night . . . lie down until the morning" (Ruth 3:13). So Ruth waited, chastely and without agitation. The next day, Naomi also advised Ruth to "wait" for future events to unfold (3:18). So Ruth waited again, with the knowledge that her future was in God's hands, not hers.

Like Ruth, the apostle Paul experienced wild oscillations between fame and rejection, hospitality and hunger, friendship and suffering, rest and restless nights. Paul revealed the secret of his contentment in a letter to friends in Philippi: "Do not worry about anything, but in everything, by prayer and supplication, with *thanksgiving*, let your requests be made known to God. And the peace of God, which surpasses all understanding, will guard your hearts and your minds in Christ Jesus" (Phil. 4:6-7, emphasis added).

Exercise

For what specifically do you need to be thankful today? Make a list and then thank God for giving you contentment with these things.

24

Life-Giving Rhythms

Struggle	Fruit	Outcome
Sloth Doing minimal or the least important work and loving ease	Faithfulness Persisting in important work with utter reliability	Life-Giving Rhythms Experiencing a pattern of life that produces excellent work without being consumed by it

PS   We've discussed that working too much, or too little, can become a form of sloth. We can also be slothful by focusing only on the urgent things without attending to important things. Marriages, families, and personal reputations have collapsed because of people's inability to prioritize important work and to do it with faithfulness.

AU   Wouldn't it be wonderful if we could produce excellent work without being consumed by it?

PS   We can do that by integrating the best of Mary and Martha, the two women who hosted Jesus in their home in Bethany. Traditionally, active Martha has been branded as a distracted and busy woman who scolded Jesus, while contemplative Mary has been praised for sitting at Jesus' feet listening attentively to him (Luke 10:39). But Martha actually did the right thing in making a meal to express love and hospitality to Jesus. Her motivations were good but her attitude was wrong.

Martha felt overcommitted and unsupported, and she held too high expectations of herself. In her dilemma she blamed God and spoiled the party for the disciples, for Jesus, and for Mary.

AU Most of us are Marthas. My colleagues and I have felt over-committed, unsupported, and harassed under demanding expectations.

PS In his love for Martha, Jesus said, "You are worried and distracted by many things; there is need of only one thing" (10:41-42). Jesus wasn't judging Martha for making a meal. In fact, Jesus probably valued Martha's hospitality. But he gently rebuked her for trying to do everything perfectly — serving a five course gourmet meal — which left her with no time for listening to and communing with him. "Mary has chosen the better part," Jesus concludes.

AU Sounds like what we really need is a combination of Mary's attitude of listening to Jesus and Martha's actions of serving Jesus.

PS That's precisely the secret to developing a life-giving rhythm that can sustain us as people who work amid today's challenges.

Work and Life-Giving Rhythms

For most people, attaining work-life balance is an elusive pursuit. It even becomes idolatrous when we seek to balance the competing demands in our life without God at the center. Instead, what we need is a life-giving rhythm that mixes together the active and reflective. This "mixed life" of action and reflection — governed by the Spirit's gift of self-control — is a wonderful corrective to the mixed-up life.

With the Spirit's gift of self-control, we will:

1. *Live a principled life governed by a rule.* For centuries, monastic communities have emphasized the value of a rule, such as the Rule of Benedict, in order to pray and work. We too can profit from living faithfully and flexibly according to a rule.

You may go about this by praying to the Holy Spirit for guidance and insight and then formulating a rhythm for yourself on a daily, weekly, and monthly basis. Resist the urge to accomplish too much; go gentle. You will discover that you won't be able to fit everything you want into your rule of life. Here you must make choices. What are the good things you must say no to in order to say yes to something better?[1] (Meeting with a spiritual director or wise friend may help you discern your *yes*es and *no*s.) Many people who live with a rule have integrated the rhythm of reading Scripture, living an examined life, keeping the Sabbath, and going on extended retreats into their lives — as laid out in the points below.

2. *Listen regularly to God's voice through the reading of Scripture and prayer.* Ever since Jesus reminded us that we do not live by bread alone, great saints through the ages have meditated on Scripture in two simple ways:

   • "Lectio continua" — Daily reading one chapter of the Old Testament starting with Genesis 1, one chapter from the New Testament starting with Matthew 1, and one psalm. In this way a person actually reads through the Bible almost once a year and the Psalms twice a year.

   • "Lectio divina" — Dwelling on one verse of Scripture by praying through it slowly, ruminating on the thoughts as a cow chews its cud, keeping silent, until God speaks.

3. *Reflect daily on what God is doing in our lives.* Great saints have practiced living an examined life in some way or form. A person who examines his or her life will instinctively or intentionally pray to God (usually at the end of the day) and ask the following questions:

   a. For what moment today am I most grateful?
   b. For what moment today am I least grateful?
   c. Review your day slowly: What are you thankful for? What do you regret?
   d. What patterns do you see occurring over the last day, week, month, or year?
   e. What do these patterns tell you about your relationship with God?

After answering these questions, weave your reflections into prayer, telling everything to God and asking God for understanding. Allow God to move you — and to surprise you, if necessary.[2]

4. *Keep the Sabbath and recognize the need for rest.* This means refraining from work, celebrating the goodness of God, and reflecting on the meaning of life. Sabbath is a law and a gift. "If you cannot afford to take one day a week for rest, you are taking yourself too seriously," says pastor and spiritual theologian Eugene Peterson.[3] Sabbath offers us the opportunity to reflect on what God has done and to receive new insights on the God for whom we are working. Sabbath prepares us for the coming week by reminding us that God is the center of all our work.

5. *Recognize the need to withdraw from busyness and activity in order to pray and reflect.* Many Christians who have understood the secret of living well realize how important it is to set aside at least two days a month for prayerful contemplation. This may also involve reading edifying books. Concentrated courses at theological schools often provide a rich context for such learning and reflection.

An Example: The Restful President

The leader of a company needs to devote a lot of time and energy to attend to people and issues. The same goes for the leader of a religious institution, who also has to live out his or her spiritual values in an authentic manner, while delivering on results and expectations. Over time, this can become exhausting, intoxicating, disorienting — or all of the above.

During the summer of 2007, Rod Wilson, the president of Regent College in Vancouver, British Columbia, a premier theological institution in North America, experienced this firsthand as he poked around the narrow streets of Hay-on-Wye in Wales. By most measures he was doing well. He had just completed a successful fundraising campaign for the construction of a new, multi-million-dollar library at Regent. The college had accrued no new debts. Students were enjoying the library. The faculty continued to support his leadership. He was also able to find time to teach and speak. The board of the college urged him to take a well-deserved summer break.

At first, Rod, an avid reader, was energized by living in Hay-on-Wye, a town of fourteen hundred people and thirty-eight used bookstores. Determined to put aside a performance-, accomplishment-, and success-oriented mind-set, Rod and his wife, Bev, stopped using a cell phone, computer, the Internet, e-mail, and a car. "We walked, read, slept, ate, talked, and moved from a lifestyle characterized by doing and performing into one that was marked by silence, contemplation, and being," Rod said.[4]

But something more happened while he was in Wales. "I experienced significant withdrawal pains, both psychologically and physically. I yearned for work and production and was troubled by having nothing to do. For me it was a significant crisis," Rod confessed. He also realized that he had been pursuing work exclusively. He had prized *doing* more than being. Sabbath had become irrelevant and insignificant to him.

"The crisis in Wales made me realize in a new way that God's economy is based on a tapestry of replenishment and work. . . . God can be seen in both the contemplative and in the active," Rod observed in retrospect. He returned to Vancouver resolved to live a new rhythm. He would be strictly religious about Sabbath, he decided. He would keep a twenty-four-hour day of rest. On that day, there would be no e-mail, Internet, or computer use of any kind. He would spend time with family or friends, or in the garden, but he would not do anything remotely related to work. One day a week, the president of Regent College would be unreachable.

Implementing the practice of Sabbath was challenging at first. People were puzzled by how Rod had become tardy in responding to e-mails sent out over the weekend. And his cell phone didn't work either. But gradually, people learned to accommodate themselves to Rod's revised schedule.

In cultivating a life-giving rhythm of rest and action, Rod had recovered more than merely well-being. He had discovered God in the center of life. "In the past eight months, I have been surprised by how the regular practice of Sabbath has produced an unexpected outcome — the deepening sense of shalom," Rod said.

Exercise

What Spirit-inspired patterns of life have been helpful to you thus far? What rhythm could you add to this? Write a plan for incorporating this new rhythm into your life.

25

Neighbor-Love

Struggle	Fruit	Outcome
Envy Feeling pain because of someone else's advancement and possessions	Kindness Putting others at ease by rejoicing in their gifts and achievements	Neighbor-Love Experiencing the ability to meet the needs of others and to contribute to their well-being

AU We've discussed how envy is deeply embedded within us. What do you think is the clearest indicator that we're no longer under the grip of envy?

PS When we're no longer preoccupied with ourselves and concerned with how we are doing. Instead, we become preoccupied with the concerns of other people — not in an obsessive or inquisitive manner — but because we desire to love and to bless them.

AU Wouldn't it make a huge difference in my workplace if I made it my goal to find creative ways to love and bless my coworkers, bosses, and staff on a daily basis?

PS That would revolutionize the workplace. Jesus summarized the whole law in the twin commandments to love God and to love neighbor. Pairing these commands means that we can love our neighbors on a long-term and sustainable basis only when we're motivated by love for God.

Work and Neighbor-Love

Envy is a sneaky, secretive sin that tries to tear people down. Henri Nouwen, the beloved author on Christian spirituality, was deeply acquainted with his proclivity toward selfish envy: "It seems easier to be God than to love God, easier to control people than to love people, easier to own life than to love life."[1]

In a wonderful contrast with envy, the love of neighbor is generous and joyful; it seeks to build people up. Instead of brooding about ourselves, we long to develop the good that is in the other. Rather than resenting it when others succeed, we rejoice.

As the Spirit increases our desire to work with love of neighbor, we will:

1. *Care for people within the organization.* We love our colleagues in the workplace when we focus on meeting their real needs. We value them first as people — regardless of their skills, competencies, or positions. We do not spend time only with like-minded people but we also look out for those who are shunned or marginalized (Luke 6:27-38; 14:12-14). In a workplace where there's little time to relate with one another, we seek to create a hospitable space where we care enough to listen to our colleagues' personal challenges.

2. *Show tough love when it is needed.* In some circumstances, acting out of love may require coaching a mediocre employee for improvement, initiating a tough conversation with a controlling boss, or reprimanding errant behavior in a team member. In other situations, acting out of love could mean the opposite: keeping silence and yielding to the other. The underlying principle is that we do whatever it takes to benefit others, not ourselves.

3. *Care for resources within the organization.* As stewards, we are called to manage the organization's assets, which include tangibles such as paper clips and photocopy machines, and intangibles such as ethics, vision, and a value system. The most important assets are people. Good stewardship requires the willingness to serve, rather than control, the people around

us, says management consultant Peter Block.[2] "The first order of business is to build a group of people who, under the influence of the institution, grow taller and become healthier and stronger," adds servant leadership guru Robert Greenleaf.[3]

4. *Care for people and resources outside the organization.* Our love for others, motivated by God's love for us, should reflect God's love for the world. In today's business parlance, this includes corporate social responsibility, through which we show loyalty toward clients, customers, suppliers, and broader stakeholders in society.[4]

Loving our neighbors near and far is a journey that lasts a lifetime, as illustrated by an ancient exchange between Basil of Caesarea and a young desert disciple:

> Once a young man went to a desert and asked the desert father for a word. The abba said, "Will you not return until you have fulfilled this word?"
>
> "I promise."
>
> "Then love the Lord your God with all your heart, soul, strength, and mind."
>
> Twenty years passed, but the young man had the temerity to come back. "I have done what you said. Now will you speak another word to me, father?"
>
> "Yes, I will but you must not return until you have fulfilled it completely."
>
> "I promise."
>
> "Then, love your neighbor as yourself."
>
> The young man never came back.[5]

An Example: The Loving Homemaker

Gladys Stevens, Paul's mother, loved her neighbor — literally.

During the long and dark Canadian winters, when Paul was a young boy, Gladys would prepare wonderful three-course meals for her husband Ernest, her two sons, and anyone who happened to be around. Invariably, Gladys would think of Albert Jupp and his aging mother, who lived in a one-room shack up the hill. Night after night Gladys would send Paul up the hill with roast beef and baked potatoes (or whatever was on the stove that night) for Albert and his mother. Gladys would also keep the outside tap open all winter so that Albert could get two pails of water each day for washing and drinking.

Gladys had grown up in a very poor family in Newfoundland. Her father was a fisherman. At sixteen she went to Toronto to earn a living as a domestic worker in the homes of wealthy people. She married Ernest and settled down to raise a family. She gave birth to three children, though the middle child was born dead. After each birth, Gladys sank into a deep depression and had to be hospitalized for weeks. In spite of this, she loved everyone in sight, whether it was relatives, strangers, or family. Paul remembers coming home from high school many times only to find that his bed or a dresser or some other large piece of furniture had disappeared — Gladys had given it to some newcomer in town. She was possibly the most generous person Paul has ever known.

Gladys had only a sixth-grade education but a wonderfully simple faith. In everything — be it reversals, opportunities, or challenges — she spoke of God with love and gratitude. That was surely the secret of her neighbor-love.

Exercise

Which of your neighbors, near or far, is most on your heart to be loved? How can you show your love to that person?

26

Vocational Confidence

Struggle	Fruit	Outcome
Restlessness Thinking and feeling that there's always something better somewhere else	Patience Having the ability to remain where you are with meaningfulness and hope	Vocational Confidence Experiencing the certainty that you are in God's will and doing God's work

AU What is one clear indicator that we are growing spiritually in our work?

PS We develop a growing confidence of God's call in our life. We are able to work with a deep certainty that whatever we are doing is aligned with God's will for us.

AU No matter what job we do? No matter how crazy or boring or meaningless?

PS Yes. We may pick a variety of jobs or pursue a single occupation. But as we grow, we become increasingly responsive to God's unique calling for us. We realize that we've been chosen by God. This gives us the confidence to work wholeheartedly, knowing that as we work, we become united with Jesus Christ.

Work and Vocational Confidence

One thing is certain: we will be in vocational transition for our whole life. This sense of transition is particularly acute for people in their twenties and thirties, who will likely work at least eight different jobs until retirement. Given that vocational transition often stirs up doubt and uncertainty, this means we need to be attuned to hear God's voice throughout our lives — and to know that times of flux and change are not necessarily bad. They offer renewed opportunity to trust in God who knows what's best for us.

As we noted in chapter 17 on patience, the Puritan William Perkins observed that all callings are equal. The calling must fit the person and the person the calling. To discern our callings, we need to explore our affections, desires, and gifts. Since we can be biased in judging our own inclinations and gifts, a robust process of discerning our calling should involve seeking advice and help from wise and trusted people. This discernment process, crucially, involves listening attentively to the One who calls us. We are not merely called to do something; we are called to unite with God.

Our calling is more than a job — it is a complete way of life. In seeking to live a called life, we will:

1. *Experience dynamic purpose and direction in our lives.* Because we are not "doing our own thing" or merely what brings us pleasure but are doing God's work, we find purpose and direction. Whether we are farming or designing a computer program, whether we are homemakers or salespeople, whether we are in the field of business or medicine, whether we are pastoring or building houses, it is truly possible for our lives and work to be in harmony with God's grand purpose of bringing about God's reign in all creation.
2. *Work and serve in love.* God does not call us to something for which we have a deep loathing. On the contrary, God's will is written into the very fiber of our lives. Our passion, our gifts and talents, the personality given to us at conception, the providential circumstances of our lives, and God speaking di-

rectly to us — these are the ingredients that help us discern where we are called to work. We are created to love work and work for love. "The important thing is not to think much, but to love much; do, then, whatever most arouses you to love," said the medieval mystic and spiritual guide, Teresa of Avila.[1]

3. *Gain a newfound confidence that we are loving our neighbor when we work.* Many workers in the twenty-first century do not see the "neighbors" they are serving. For example, lab technicians, computer programmers, copy editors, kitchen staff, and other people who work behind the scenes do not meet the customers or stakeholders they are serving. Nonetheless, if we discern that we are called to the work, and if we sense that this work is meeting a deeply felt need in the wider community, then we are indeed loving our neighbors with our work. Frederick Buechner, a contemporary Christian author, expresses this elegantly: "The kind of work God usually calls you to is the kind of work that you need most to do and the world most needs to have done. . . . Thus, the place God calls you is the place your deep gladness and the world's deep hunger meet."[2]

4. *Discover that work has not only intrinsic value* (is worth doing for itself, not just for the pay) but may well have endurance and find its place in the new earth that God will be remaking.

5. *Experience God at work within us.* God is shaping, molding, and renewing us as we work, thus bringing us into a deeper union and fellowship with God. Just as our lives are works in progress, our occupations are works in progress. And our life with God is also in progress while we work.

An Example: The Called Merchant

Calvin Seerveld, a Canadian theologian, tells the story of his father, owner of a fish shop at the Great South Bay Fish Market in New York. The shop smelled like fish. It was always a bustling, happy place to work, with lots of laughter. As a young boy, Calvin worked there.

One day, on a busy Friday afternoon, Calvin watched his father trying to convince a reluctant customer — a prosperous woman from the neighborhood — that the carp was a good buy. Merchant and customer both scrutinized the fish. Using his beefy hands, Calvin's father raised the fish into the light. The fish's eyes were bright. The gills had good color. The flesh was firm. As the woman gazed at the beautiful fish, her resistance crumbled. The price seemed right.

"Beautiful!" exclaimed Calvin's father. "Shall I clean it up for you?"

The woman assented. She noted ruefully how smoothly the deal was struck. "My, you certainly didn't miss your calling," she told Calvin's father.

In reflecting on this boyhood moment, Seerveld observed that the woman had inadvertently spoken the truth about his father. "My father was in full-time service for the Lord, prophet, priest, and king in the fish business, consecratedly cutting up fish for the glory of God," Seerveld wrote.[3]

Exercise

How wonderful it would be if more of us had a strong sense of vocational confidence in the work we do. Do you? If not, consider developing a process that will help you discern God's calling in your life.

27

Practical Heavenly-Mindedness

Struggle	Fruit	Outcome
Boredom Having insufficient passion or interest to give yourself heartily to work and life	Peace Having a passion for completeness and harmony, no matter what the situation	Heavenly-Mindedness Experiencing the meaning and joy of work that will last in view of eternity

AU Do you think our work done on earth will survive in heaven?

PS This question interests me deeply because I am now at the stage of life when many of my dearest friends and family have died, and I myself am aging. I think of two lines from a poem that says,

> Only one life, 'twill soon be passed.
> Only what's done for Christ will last.

It's not our role to figure out what kind of work will survive in heaven. Nothing we do in itself will last. But we can rest assured that work that is carried out with faith, hope, and love — done for the sake of Jesus Christ — will somehow find its place in the new heaven and new earth.

AU Will I find in heaven the kayak that you built for your grandchildren?

PS I'm not sure whether the books I've written will survive the purging of God's holy fire. But I really hope you'll see the kayak in heaven. I built it out of love.

Work and Heavenly-Mindedness

There's a saying that people can be too heavenly-minded to be of any earthly use. But the reality is that authentic heavenly-mindedness is the most practical thing on earth. The Puritans, for example, were skilled administrators and artisans who stressed the importance of living each day with the knowledge that we will die and that there's an art in learning how to die well. In contrast, many people these days live as if death is not a part of reality.

Having a sense of one's mortality can often be construed as being despairing. Certain cultures even consider talk of death to be taboo or bad luck. And yet such a seemingly morbid worldview is a truly biblical mind-set that points us to the reality of heaven. "Set your minds on things that are above, not on things that are on earth," Paul advised (Col. 3:2). In the same way, John Baillie, a pastor, used to pray: "O Lord, grant that each day I may do something so to strengthen my hold upon the unseen world . . . that as the end of my earthly life draws ever nearer, I may grow more and more conformed to the life of the world to come."[1]

Having practical heavenly-mindedness is the only way to make ultimate sense out of life in this world. C. S. Lewis, the Oxford don and Christian apologist, said, "Aim at heaven and you will get earth thrown in; aim at earth and you will get neither."[2]

When we work with heavenly-mindedness, we will:

1. *Gain an eternal perspective on why we work.* One day, we will enter into the joy of the master (Matt. 25:21). In the meanwhile, we live and work like the servants in Jesus' parables, who labored diligently because they knew that their master would one day return.
2. *Gain a cosmic understanding of our personal calling.* Our calling or vocation does not cease with retirement or even with

death. In some mysterious but marvelous way, our specific calling will continue into the new heaven and new earth.

3. *Gain hope and courage in overcoming all kinds of obstacles — be they external or internal.* We will not lose hope because we are told again and again in Revelation, the last book of the Bible, how Jesus has already overcome all obstacles. He will usher in the perfect reign of God and bring perfect order and harmony to everything.

4. *Care for our planet and its environment.* Our planet will somehow last for eternity and be transfigured by the Sovereign God. We work with an authentic hope that the fruit of our work will endure in the "new heaven and new earth" (Rev. 21:1). Catholic theologian Yves Congar observes that "final salvation will be achieved by a wonderful refloating of our earthly vessel rather than the transfer of the survivors to another ship wholly built by God."[3]

5. *Know that the work we do in this world (whether manual or mental) has intrinsic value.* The resurrection of Christ has conquered death and given us the hope that our work, purged of sin and renewed by God, will somehow find its place in the new heaven and new earth. Just as "earth's crammed with heaven,"[4] heaven is also crammed with earth. "When the final consummation comes, the work you have done, whether in Bible study or biochemistry, whether in preaching or in pure mathematics, whether in digging ditches or in composing symphonies, will stand, will last," writes Bible scholar N. T. Wright.[5]

An Example: The Heavenly-Minded Prisoner

On a rocky outcropping off the Island of Patmos, an old man stood and watched the dark gray waters of the Aegean Sea churning below. By rights, he should have been in chains, for he was a prisoner sentenced to exile by the Roman authorities for subversive activities as a follower of Jesus Christ. But his guards had taken pity on him. He was a harmless old man, they said.

166

So John the Beloved was allowed to walk around the barren island without chains. He had been here a long time. There wasn't anywhere else to go. He spent most of his waking hours writing letters. Or he'd sit still, eyes closed, dozing in the sunlight. At least, that was what the guards thought. But John was seeing and experiencing life on an entirely different plane of reality. The past, the present, and eternity existed as one. For John had a secret nobody else knew: as a young man, he had heard the heartbeat of eternity.

Fifty years ago, he had befriended Jesus of Nazareth. John had loved Jesus the moment they met. For three shimmering years, John belonged to the Twelve who traveled everywhere with Jesus. One night, before the terrible events had unfolded, John was in the upper room in Jerusalem eating supper with Jesus and the rest of the Twelve. Out of great affection for his friend, John had laid his head against Jesus' chest. Hours later, in Gethsemane, John overheard Jesus pray to God, calling God his "Father." These were two small moments in an amazing series of events that unfolded: Jesus crucified, Jesus buried, Jesus bursting into life from the grave, and Jesus ascending bodily into heaven.

It had taken John the Beloved several more years of prayerful reflection before he realized the staggering truth: Jesus, his Palestinian friend who spoke Aramaic, who died and rose again, was also the eternal Word who had created the heavens and the earth. Therefore, when John laid his head on Jesus' chest, he had heard the heartbeat of eternity beating. In touching Jesus, John had touched Eternal Life. In listening to Jesus pray, John was listening to a conversation between God the Father and God the Son.

Now, on Patmos, John reflected on his life. He was, at heart, a very practical man. He had pastored many churches in Asia Minor. He had counseled troubled souls. He had shared firsthand insights with new believers. But he knew that what would sustain their faith would not be fundraising campaigns, membership drives, or seeker-sensitive worship services. John saw a different reality. He saw the Spirit's mighty work. He saw the final victory of the slain Lamb sitting on the throne — Jesus Christ, who has overcome all oppressive regimes and seductive powers for all eternity. He saw a totally transfigured heaven, a renewed earth. Nothing would ever be the same because of the man whose heartbeat he had heard.

Yes, John's eyes were closed. But he was not dozing. As a prisoner for Christ, stuck on a wind-blasted rock, John knew there was one thing he could do to encourage believers facing severe oppression or terrible discouragement as they work. He would find a way to convince future generations of believers of a new way to live — to adopt a heavenly mind-set.

In a culture openly hostile or seductively friendly to the Christian faith, John was convinced that the only way we can work with integrity is to discover a heavenly reality. And the most important cosmic fact is this: Through the cross, Jesus has already overcome Satan and his allies. Jesus Christ, the perfect human being, is seated on the throne, the King of kings and Lord of lords.

John knew that this vision of heaven and of Christ triumphant would sear the imaginations of jaded Christians who live compromised lives in the workplace. John also knew that our work in this world, whether manual, mental, or spiritual, will endure forever if we do it for the sake of the risen Christ. Jesus himself had told John so: "I am making all things new" (Rev. 21:5).

Not least, John knew that the deepest joy we can anticipate is meeting the risen Jesus face-to-face — to know God as God knows us. Such heavenly knowledge transformed John. In some way, John knew instinctively that this would transform you and me.

Exercise

Your work will somehow last and be continued in the new heaven and new earth. List the ways in which this knowledge can impact your approach and attitude toward your work.

EPILOG

One Last Conversation on What It Means to Grow Spiritually in the Workplace

Two motorboats bob in the water. One of them is Paul's — the one that will bring us back to civilization.

For three days, we have lived in a cabin on the anvil-shaped Ruxton Island with no running water, no electricity, and no Internet access. The power for our laptops, which we have been using to write this book, is generated by the sun. The water we drink is pumped from a well. The heat that warms us radiates from a wood stove. After sundown, the silence that settles into the night is thick — like a wool blanket that has descended from the heavens and engulfed this small hand-built cabin in the vastness of the Canadian Gulf Islands.

At first blush, Ruxton Island seems like the last place on earth you would go to complete a book on the spirituality of work. A book on work should be written in the buzz of a city, perhaps in Vancouver or Kuala Lumpur, where we live. But here we are — along with our respective wives — editing the final drafts of the book in one of the most tranquil spots on earth.

You don't come to Ruxton to make a living. There are no businesses here: no ice-cream shop, hot-dog stand, bar, or local restaurant. You come to Ruxton to relax and retreat from the world. You come here to read. You come here to get away from people. Decades ago, a hippie came here to live off the land. He cultivated a small farm behind his cabin. He raised chickens. He grew beans, potatoes, and squash in the shallow topsoil. He also grew his hair long. But since his death a few years ago, all trace of the farm and any evidence of the work of his hands have been swallowed up.

Yet if we look closely enough, even on Ruxton Island, the world of work is close at hand. At any moment, in any place, someone — or something — is hard at work. Spend a few minutes on a quiet Saturday afternoon walking with us along the rugged shoreline:

You'll see the sun's rays breaking through dark masses of clouds. A slight northwesterly wind is churning up the water, causing ripple after ripple to flow into the bay, pushing seawater into the tide pools. Idle seaweeds, plastered against rock, suddenly burst into life, waving their green arms in sync with the swirling water. Purple starfish, hunting for oysters, creep along the rocks. Small fish dart in and out of nooks and crannies, looking for food, or to escape from becoming food. Hermit crabs drag their homes with them like backpackers looking for odd jobs. This tiny acreage at your feet is full of marine animals hard at work — hunting, hiding, digging, tugging, foraging, and feeding. These activities are being replicated throughout the island, on land, across the sea, and in the air, where the seagulls pinwheel and the eagles fly. Through creation, we see a million glimpses of God at work.

Open your eyes: God is on the move.

God is on the move, not just on a quiet beach on Ruxton Island, but perhaps much more so in a multistory office block, a factory production line, a woodshop, a classroom, or a kitchen. God is at work wherever people are working. God is at work through all of us. Our entire lives are also works in progress. Through work, we are progressing toward God.

In writing and editing this book together, we have seen God working in our lives. We wish you this same joy of discovering God at work in your life. In the same way we've been enriched by our conversations with one another, we hope you'll find a friend with whom you can start a conversation on what it means to be growing spiritually in the workplace. Meanwhile, we invite you to eavesdrop on our final conversation.

PS   We're nearly done with our conversations on growing spiritually while we work. Through our discussions, I've learned that even simply watering plants in my apartment can be a seamless experience of working for God and with God. What have you learned?

AU   I've learned that the workplace is a playground for learning to love God and to love people. As at any playground, I can get into scrapes. There could even be a neighborhood bully. But it's also in the playground that I make friends and learn to play and work with them. I learn to experiment. In the same way, there's no better place than the workplace to put into practice the ideas and guiding principles we've discussed in this book. As I can at a playground, I can try new things at work every day, such as learning to be thankful for struggles, or treating people with gentleness, or working with a heavenly mind-set. I've also been discovering the importance of living within my limitations.

PS   Living within your limitations — what does that mean for you?

AU   We all like to see ourselves as human beings with limitless potential. But the danger is that we could ignore our dark sides. And that can really hurt us. For example, ever since I was young, I've always wanted people to admire my intelligence and to lap up every word that I say. So I'm willing to do whatever it takes — even work to the point of exhaustion or neglect of loved ones — to please people who think highly of my teaching or speaking. I'm driven to take on leadership positions in churches and Christian organizations, not because I primarily want to serve people, but because I want people to admire me. The ancient teachers of spirituality labeled such behavior as "vainglory," a form of pride. The problem with vainglory is that I deceive myself into thinking that I am glorifying God with my work when in reality I am subtly trying to impress people. The danger with working solely with my strengths is that I end up with an inflated sense of self. On the other hand, when I live within my limitations, I discover new God-given strengths.

PS   And how does the workplace teach you about working through your limitations?

AU In all the jobs I've taken on so far, I've been drawn to new challenges. During the learning process though, I have often felt ignorant, incompetent, and stupid. But, I've also discovered the redemptive side of living within my limitations. They safeguard me from being inflated with vainglory. Because I'm trying to survive at work, I'm not thinking of impressing anybody. More importantly, in my weakness, I realize that God is helping me. And it fills me with joy and gratitude.

PS In other words, your struggles in the workplace are potentially an avenue for the Spirit's blessing.

AU Absolutely. We all face debilitating spiritual struggles when we work. Therefore it's important to identify the struggles so that we can surrender them to God. Then we'll discover that the Holy Spirit empowers us to work in a radical new way. Unwittingly, and in an unselfconscious manner, we become more and more like Jesus Christ. God makes something beautiful from even the most soul-sapping struggle.

PS How true. For me, work has become an arena to know myself. I see myself struggling with drivenness. But over time, God has been healing me from this drive to perform and become more productive.

AU I've definitely appreciated working with you. You always take time to catch up with me on personal matters over coffee, yet you're very effective in getting things done. Do you think that a deeper understanding of workplace spirituality has made you more effective in doing your work?

PS Possibly, but that would not be its main purpose. Spirituality is not a motivational technique for reviving tired workers. It is not a three-step Christian program for getting things done. Christian spirituality is far more subversive. It's the Spirit of God working to transform us from within; our inner transformation then affects everything we do and why we do it.

AU Would you say then that one indicator that we're growing spiritually is that we become excellent at our work?

PS In a way, yes. We don't pursue excellence as the ultimate goal. But because we know that we are serving God and doing our Sovereign's work, we feel motivated to do the best we can. We want our work to be "something beautiful for God." At the same time, sometimes we have to do certain things less than perfectly simply because the limitations we face in time and resources do not permit us to complete them to perfection.

AU The key thing is that we're keeping company with God while we work. I think it was Cardinal Wyszyński who said that if we love God, it is impossible not to tell God so when we are working.

PS Indeed. We will have more depth and sensitivity to the Spirit's leading as we experience God in the workplace.

AU Does that mean that God will also help us achieve a perfect work-life balance?

PS You're pulling my leg, aren't you? You know that I don't believe in work-life balance. That's not the key question in growing spiritually while we work. The key questions are these: How do we keep company with Jesus Christ while we work? And how does God keep company with us while we work? When we ask these two questions throughout our lives, we'll always discover something new to learn.

AU You're right. When we are aware that we are working with God, and God is working with us, the issue of work-life balance fades in the background.

PS That's because we're not distinguishing between "work" and "life." Rather, because God is in the center of all things, all of life is sacred.

AU And when we discover that God is in the center of everything, there is true balance.

Notes

Introduction

1. Quoted in Eric Steven Dale, *Bringing Heaven Down to Earth: A Practical Spirituality of Work* (New York: Peter Lang, 1991), p. 8.

2. Gregory F. A. Pierce, *Spirituality at Work: 10 Ways to Balance Your Life on the Job* (Chicago: Loyola Press, 2001), p. 18.

Part One — Nine Soul-Sapping Struggles in the Workplace: Introducing the Deadly Work Sins

1. Quoted in William H. Willimon, *Sinning Like a Christian: A New Look at the Seven Deadly Sins* (Nashville: Abingdon Press, 2005), p. 21.

Chapter 1 — Pride: Grasping Equality with God

1. Bernard of Clairvaux, *Selected Works,* trans. G. R. Evans (New York: Paulist Press, 1987), p. 100.

2. Bernard of Clairvaux, *Selected Works,* p. 103.

3. Michael Casey, *A Guide to Living in the Truth: Saint Benedict's Teaching on Humility* (Liguori, Mo.: Liguori, 2001), p. 174.

Chapter 2 — Greed: The Desire for More

1. Donald J. Trump, "The Fourth Deadly Workplace Sin: Greed," The Trump

Blog, entry posted October 8, 2007, http://www.trumpuniversity.com/blog/post/2007/10/the-fourth-deadly-workplace-sin-greed.cfm (accessed October 12, 2008).

2. Paul Jordan-Smith, "Seven (and more) Deadly Sins," *Parabola* 10 (Winter 1985): 41.

3. Alexander Schmemann, *For the Life of the World: Sacraments and Orthodoxy* (Crestwood, N.Y.: St. Vladimir's Seminary Press, 1973), pp. 11, 18.

4. Richard Pollay and R. Paul Stevens, "Advertising," in Robert Banks and R. Paul Stevens, eds., *The Complete Book of Everyday Christianity* (Downers Grove, Ill.: InterVarsity Press, 1997), p. 26. Approximately one hundred fifty of the articles from *The Complete Book* are available free and can be copied from the following website: www.ivmdl.org/cbec.cfm. *The Complete Book* can be purchased in its entirety in soft copy (CD-ROM) along with other Bible resources, from the Internet. See www.bible-explorer.com.

5. John Wesley, "The Use of Money," in Max L. Stackhouse et al., *On Moral Business: Classical and Contemporary Resources for Ethics in Economic Life* (Grand Rapids: Eerdmans, 1995), pp. 194-97.

6. Dennis W. Bakke, *Joy at Work: A Revolutionary Approach to Fun on the Job* (Toronto: Viking, 2005).

Chapter 3 — Lust: The Erotic Workplace

1. Karl A. Olsson, *Seven Sins and Seven Virtues* (New York: Harper & Brothers, 1962), p. 54.

2. Richard Rohr, "An Appetite for Wholeness," *Sojourners*, November 1982), p. 30.

3. John Piper, "Battling the Unbelief of Lust," desiringGod, http://www.desiringgod.org/ResourceLibrary/sermons/bydate/1988/657_Battling_the_Unbelief_of_Lust/ (accessed October 12, 2008).

4. Quoted in Stanford M. Lyman, *The Seven Deadly Sins and Evil* (Dix Hills, N.Y.: General Hall, Inc., 1989), p. 55.

5. Wendy Tuohy, "Love in a corporate climate," The Age, http://www.theage.com.au/articles/2003/07/25/1059084206429.html (accessed September 3, 2008).

6. Matthew the Poor, *Orthodox Prayer Life: The Interior Way* (Crestwood, N.Y.: St. Vladimir's Seminary Press, 2003), p. 118.

7. Willimon, *Sinning Like a Christian*, p. 145.

Chapter 4 — Gluttony: Excessive Consumption of Food

1. Leon R. Kass, *The Hungry Soul: Eating and the Perfecting of Our Nature* (Chicago: University of Chicago Press, 1994), pp. 89-90.

175

2. Gregory I, *Moralia*, XXX, 18, quoted in Gerard Reed, *C. S. Lewis Explores Vice and Virtue* (Kansas City: Beacon Hill Press, 2001), pp. 62-63.

3. C. S. Lewis, *The Screwtape Letters*, ch. 24, quoted in Willimon, *Sinning Like a Christian*, p. 122.

4. Quoted in Olsson, *Seven Sins and Seven Virtues*, p. 50.

Chapter 5 — Anger: The Burning Desire to Control

1. Stanley Bing, *Sun Tzu Was a Sissy: Conquer Your Enemies, Promote Your Friends, and the Real Art of Wage War* (New York: HarperCollins, 2004), p. 89.

2. Tomas Spidlik, *The Spirituality of the Christian East: A Systematic Handbook* (Kalamazoo, Mich.: Cistercian Publications, 1986), p. 250.

3. John Cassian, *The Conferences*, trans. Boniface Ramsey (New York: Paulist Press, 1997), p. 566.

4. Cassian, *The Conferences*, p. 569.

5. Cassian, *The Conferences*, p. 569.

6. Cassian, *The Conferences*, p. 570.

7. Cassian, *The Conferences*, p. 574.

Chapter 6 — Sloth: Pathological Busyness

1. Donald J. Trump, "The Fifth Deadly Workplace Sin: Sloth," The Trump Blog, entry posted October 10, 2007, http://www.trumpuniversity.com/blog/post/2007/10/the-fifth-deadly-workplace-sin-sloth.cfm (accessed October 7, 2008).

2. Derek Kidner, *The Proverbs: An Introduction and Commentary* (Downers Grove, Ill.: InterVarsity Press, 1975), pp. 42-43.

3. Sylvia Ann Hewlett and Carolyn Buck Luce, "Extreme Jobs: The Dangerous Allure of the 70-Hour Week," *Harvard Business Review* (December 2006): 49-59.

4. Frederick Buechner, *Wishful Thinking: A Seeker's ABC*, rev. and expanded ed. (San Francisco: HarperSanFrancisco, 1993), pp. 109-10.

5. Francis de Sales, *Introduction to the Devout Life*, trans. and ed. John K. Ryan (New York: Image Books, 2003), p. 202.

6. de Sales, *Introduction to the Devout Life*, p. 201.

7. R. Paul Stevens, "Drivenness," in Banks and Stevens, eds., *The Complete Book of Everyday Christianity*, pp. 312-18.

Chapter 7 — Envy: The Pain of Another's Advancement

1. Buechner, *Wishful Thinking*, p. 24.

2. Cited in Elaine Jarvik, "Envy — Sin that's 'no fun at all' has elements

of pride, greed, anger," *Deseret News*, http://www.deseretnews.com/article/
1,5143,635197503,00.html (accessed August 1, 2008).

3. Quoted in Jarvik, "Envy."

Chapter 8 — Restlessness: The Desire to Run Away

1. For Evagrius there were eight rather than seven deadly sins.

2. William Harmless, *Desert Christians: An Introduction to the Literature of Early Monasticism* (Oxford: Oxford University Press, 2004), p. 325.

3. Augustine of Hippo, *Selected Writings*, trans. Mary T. Clark (Mahwah, N.J.: Paulist Press, 1984), p. 9.

4. Anthony C. Meisel and M. L. del Mastro, trans., *The Rule of Saint Benedict* (New York: Doubleday, 1975), p. 47.

5. Esther de Waal, *A Life-Giving Way: A Commentary on the Rule of St. Benedict* (Collegeville, Minn.: Liturgical Press, 1995), p. 189.

6. de Sales, *Introduction to the Devout Life*, p. 205.

Chapter 9 — Boredom: Slow Death in the Workplace

1. O. E. Klapp, *Overload and Boredom* (Westport, Conn.: Greenwood, 1986), p. 20.

2. S. D. Healy, *Boredom, Self, and Culture* (Cranbury, N.J.: Associate University Presses, 1984), p. 17.

3. Blaise Pascal, *Pensées*, trans. A. J. Krailsheimer (London: Penguin Classics, 1995), p. 40.

4. Quoted in R. Paul Stevens, "Boredom," in Banks and Stevens, eds., *The Complete Book of Everyday Christianity*, p. 83.

5. Pascal, *Pensées*, p. 119.

Part Two — Nine Life-Giving Resources for Workplace Spirituality: Introducing the Spirit's Fruit

1. Evelyn Underhill, *The Fruits of the Spirit* (Wilton, Conn.: Morehouse-Barlow Co., 1981), p. 13.

2. Underhill, *The Fruits of the Spirit*, p. 50.

Chapter 10 — Joy: More Than Happiness at Work

1. William Barclay, *Flesh and Spirit: An Examination of Galatians 5:19-23* (London: SCM, 1962), p. 77.
2. Bakke, *Joy at Work*, p. 44.
3. Michael Ruhlman, *Wooden Boats: In Pursuit of the Perfect Craft at an American Boatyard* (New York: Penguin Books, 2001), p. 237.

Chapter 11 — Goodness: Unselfconscious Giving

1. 2 Thess. 2:17; Eph. 5:9; Rom. 15:14.
2. Barclay, *Flesh and Spirit*, p. 105.
3. John M. Drescher, *Doing What Comes Spiritually* (Scottdale, Pa.: Herald Press, 1993), p. 231.
4. Thomas Aquinas, "Treatise on Faith, Hope, and Charity," *Summa Theologica,* Part II of second part, Q. 32, Art. 2.
5. William E. Diehl and Judith R. Diehl, *It Ain't Over Till It's Over: A User's Guide to the Second Half of Life* (Minneapolis: Augsburg, 2003), pp. 129-30.

Chapter 12 — Love: The Greatest Thing to Give and Receive

1. R. Paul Stevens, *The Other Six Days: Vocation, Work, and Ministry in Biblical Perspective* (Grand Rapids: Eerdmans, 2000), p. 103.
2. Gerald Bray, ed., *James, 1-2 Peter, 1-3 John, Jude,* Ancient Christian Commentary on Scripture, New Testament, vol. 11 (Downers Grove, Ill.: InterVarsity Press, 2000), pp. 194-95.
3. Underhill, *The Fruits of the Spirit*, p. 14.
4. Underhill, *The Fruits of the Spirit*, pp. 14-15.
5. For a comprehensive list of attributes of *hesed,* see K. Lawson Younger Jr., *Judges, Ruth,* The NIV Application Commentary (Grand Rapids: Zondervan, 2002), p. 394.
6. Dallas Willard, *Renovation of the Heart* (Colorado Springs: Navpress, 2002), p. 132.

Chapter 13 — Self-Control: Resolving the Work-Life Dilemma

1. Edward M. Hallowell, "Overloaded Circuits: Why Smart People Underperform," *Harvard Business Review on Bringing Your Whole Self to Work* (Boston: Harvard Business School Press, 2008), pp. 1-3.

2. "Work-life balance," Wikipedia, http://en.wikipedia.org/wiki/Work_life
_balance (accessed October 9, 2008).

3. John Dalla Costa, *Magnificence at Work: Living Faith in Business* (Toronto: Novalis, 2005), p. 67.

4. Dalla Costa, *Magnificence at Work*, p. 34.

Chapter 14 — Gentleness: The Strength of Meekness

1. Ps. 18:35; 37:11; Isa. 40:11; Zech. 9:9; Matt. 5:5; 11:29-30; 12:20; 1 Cor. 4:21; 2 Cor. 10:1; Gal. 5:22-23, 6:1; Eph. 4:2; Col. 3:12; 1 Thess. 2:7; 1 Tim. 3:3, 6:11; 2 Tim. 2:25; Titus 3:2; Heb. 5:2; James 3:13; 3:17; 1 Pet. 5:6.

2. Judith C. Lechman, *The Spirituality of Gentleness: Growing toward Christian Wholeness* (San Francisco: Harper & Row, 1987), p. 146.

3. "Some Sayings of the Desert Fathers," Villanova University, http://www29.homepage.villanova.edu/christopher.haas/saying%20of%20the%20desert%20fathers.html (accessed August 12, 2008).

4. Gary L. Thomas, "Choosing gentleness: A gentle spirit gives the world a taste of the presence of Jesus," *Discipleship Journal* 18, no. 6 (Nov./Dec. 1998): 43-48.

Chapter 15 — Faithfulness: Workplace Integrity

1. M. Mitchell Waldrop, "Dee Hock on Management: Dee Hock's management principles, in his own words," *Fast Company* 5 (October 1996): 79.

2. Barclay, *Flesh and Spirit*, p. 111.

3. Barclay, *Flesh and Spirit*, pp. 110-11.

4. Stephen L. Carter, *Integrity* (New York: Basic Books, 1996), quoted in David W. Gill, "No Integrity, No Trust; No Trust, No Business," *Ethix: The Bulletin of the Institute for Business, Technology, and Ethics* 14 (August 2000): 11.

5. Stefan Cardinal Wyszyński, *All You Who Labor: Work and the Sanctification of Daily Life* (Manchester, N.H.: Sophia Institute Press, 1995), p. 113.

Chapter 16 — Kindness: Putting Others at Ease

1. Jean Vanier, *Community and Growth*, trans. Jean Vanier (New York: Paulist Press, 1989), p. 267.

2. Barclay, *Flesh and Spirit*, p. 97.

3. Barclay, *Flesh and Spirit*, p. 101.

4. Edgar H. Schein, *Organizational Culture and Leadership: A Dynamic View* (San Francisco: Jossey-Bass, 1991), p. 6.

5. Schein, *Organizational Culture and Leadership*, pp. 191, 241.

Chapter 17 — Patience: Remaining Where You Are with Hope

1. Underhill, *The Fruits of the Spirit*, p. 25.
2. Wyszyński, *All You Who Labor*, pp. 123, 141.
3. William Perkins, *The Works of That Famous Minister of Christ in the University of Cambridge* (London: John Legatt, 1626).
4. Perkins, *The Works of That Famous Minister of Christ*, p. 758.
5. Benedicta Ward, SLG, trans., *The Sayings of the Desert Fathers: The Alphabetical Collection* (London: Cistercian Publications, 1985), p. 2.

Chapter 18 — Peace: Bringing Wholeness and Harmony

1. Eugene Peterson and Anneke Kaai, *In a Word* (Brewster, Mass.: Paraclete Press, 2003), p. 50.
2. Buechner, *Wishful Thinking*, p. 83.
3. Barclay, *Flesh and Spirit*, p. 87.
4. Manlio Simetti, ed., *Matthew 1-13*, Ancient Christian Commentary on Scripture, New Testament, vol. 1a (Downers Grove, Ill.: InterVarsity Press, 2001), p. 204.
5. Gerald Bray, ed., *Romans*, Ancient Christian Commentary on Scripture, New Testament, vol. 6 (Downers Grove, Ill.: InterVarsity Press, 1998), p. 126.

Chapter 19 — Continuous Prayer

1. Wyszyński, *All You Who Labor*, p. 73.
2. Sadhu Sundar Singh, *With and Without Christ* (London: Cassell and Co., 1929), p. 74.
3. Adapted from Brother Lawrence, *The Practice of the Presence of God* (Grand Rapids: Spire, 1967), p. 19.
4. Adapted from Lawrence, *The Practice of the Presence of God*, p. 19.
5. Adapted from Lawrence, *The Practice of the Presence of God*, p. 22.

Chapter 20 — Persistent Gratitude

1. Schmemann, *For the Life of the World*, pp. 11, 18.
2. Donald P. McNeill, Douglas A. Morrison, and Henri J. M. Nouwen, *Compassion: A Reflection on the Christian Life* (Garden City, N.Y.: Doubleday, 1982), p. 126.

Chapter 21 — Beautiful Purity

1. Søren Kierkegaard, *Purity of Heart Is to Will One Thing* (New York: Harper & Brothers, 1948), p. 31.

2. Mother Teresa, *Total Surrender* (Ann Arbor, Mich.: Servant Publications, 1985), pp. 26, 38.

3. John Cassian, *Conferences,* trans. Colm Luibheid (New York: Paulist Press, 1985), p. 129.

Chapter 22 — Joyful Relinquishment

1. Jacob Needleman, *Money and the Meaning of Life* (New York: Doubleday, 1991), p. 112.

2. Julie and Robert Banks, "Simpler Lifestyle," in Banks and Stevens, eds., *The Complete Book of Everyday Christianity,* pp. 896-900.

3. John Wesley, "The Use of Money," in Stackhouse et al., eds., *On Moral Business,* pp. 194-97.

4. William E. Diehl, *Thank God It's Monday* (Philadelphia: Fortress Press, 1982), p. 133.

Chapter 23 — Surrendered Contentment

1. Jean-Pierre de Caussade, *The Sacrament of the Present Moment,* trans. Kitty Muggeridge (Glasgow: Silliam Collins & Co., 1987), p. 117.

2. Mother Teresa, *No Greater Love* (Maryknoll, N.Y.: New World Library, 1997), pp. 148-49.

3. de Caussade, *The Sacrament of the Present Moment,* p. 84.

4. François Fénelon, *The Royal Way of the Cross,* ed. Hal Helms (Brewster, Mass.: Paraclete, 1982), p. 31.

5. Fenelon, *The Royal Way of the Cross,* p. 27.

Chapter 24 — Life-Giving Rhythms

1. Adapted from M. Basil Pennington, *A School of Love: The Cistercian Way to Holiness* (Harrisburg, Pa.: Morehouse, 2000), p. 9.

2. Tim Muldoon, *The Ignatian Workout: Daily Spiritual Exercises for a Healthy Faith* (Chicago: Loyola Press, 2004), pp. 42-43.

3. Eugene Peterson, "The Pastor's Sabbath," *Leadership* (Spring 1985): 55-56.

4. Rod Wilson, "Shabbat and Shalom," *The Regent World* 20, no. 2 (Winter 2008): 1.

Chapter 25 — Neighbor-Love

1. Henri J. M. Nouwen, *In the Name of Jesus: Reflections on Christian Leadership* (New York: Crossroad, 1993), pp. 59-60.

2. Peter Block, *Stewardship: Choosing Service over Self-Interest* (San Francisco: Berrett-Koehler, 1993), p. 22.

3. Quoted in Block, *Stewardship*, p. 22. Also see Chris Lowney, *Heroic Leadership: Best Practices from a 450-Year-Old Company that Changed the World* (Chicago: Loyola Press, 2003), p. 169.

4. Donald E. Flow, "Profit," in Banks and Stevens, eds., *The Complete Book of Everyday Christianity*, pp. 812-13.

5. Benedicta Ward, SLG, trans., *The Sayings of the Desert Fathers*, p. xxii.

Chapter 26 — Vocational Confidence

1. Teresa of Avila, *Interior Castle*, trans. Allison Peers (New York: Doubleday, 1989), p. 76.

2. Buechner, *Wishful Thinking*, p. 398.

3. Calvin Seerveld, *Christian Workers, Unite!* (Toronto: Christian Labour Association of Canada, 1964), pp. 7-8.

Chapter 27 — Practical Heavenly-Mindedness

1. John Baillie, *A Diary of Private Prayer* (London: Oxford University Press, 1958), p. 129.

2. Quoted in R. Paul Stevens and Michael Green, *Living the Story: Biblical Spirituality for Everyday Christians* (Grand Rapids: Eerdmans, 2003), p. 176.

3. Yves Congar, *Lay People in the Church: A Study for a Theology of the Laity*, trans. D. Attwater (Westminster, Md.: Newman Press, 1957), p. 92.

4. Elizabeth Barrett Browning, quoted in Elizabeth A. Dreyer, *Earth Crammed with Heaven: A Spirituality of Everyday Life* (New York: Paulist Press, 1994), p. 1.

5. N. T. Wright, *The Challenge of Jesus: Rediscovering Who Jesus Was and Is* (Downers Grove, Ill.: InterVarsity Press, 1999), pp. 180-81.

Bibliography

Alford, Helen J., and Michael J. Naughton. *Managing as If Faith Mattered: Christian Social Principles in the Modern Organization.* Notre Dame, Ind.: Notre Dame University Press, 2001.

Allegretti, Joseph G. *Loving Your Job, Finding Your Passion: Work and the Spiritual Life.* New York: Paulist Press, 2000.

Anderson, Ray S. *The Shape of Practical Theology: Empowering Ministry with Theological Praxis.* Downers Grove, Ill.: InterVarsity Press, 2001.

Aquinas, Thomas. "Treatise on Faith, Hope, and Charity." *Summa Theologica,* Part II of second part, Q. 32, Art. 2.

Augustine of Hippo. *Selected Writings.* Translated by Mary T. Clark. Mahwah, N.J.: Paulist Press, 1984.

Baillie, John. *A Diary of Private Prayer.* London: Oxford University Press, 1958.

Bakke, Dennis W. *Joy at Work: A Revolutionary Approach to Fun on the Job.* Toronto: Viking, 2005.

Banks, Julie, and Robert Banks. "Simpler Lifestyle." In *The Complete Book of Everyday Christianity,* edited by Robert Banks and R. Paul Stevens, pp. 896-900. Downers Grove, Ill.: InterVarsity Press, 1997.

Banks, Robert. *The Tyranny of Time: When 24 Hours Is Not Enough.* Downers Grove, Ill.: InterVarsity Press, 1983.

Banks, Robert, and R. Paul Stevens, eds. *The Complete Book of Everyday Christianity.* Downers Grove, Ill.: InterVarsity Press, 1997.

Barclay, William. *Flesh and Spirit: An Examination of Galatians 5:19-23.* London: SCM, 1962.

Bernard of Clairvaux. *Selected Works.* Translated by G. R. Evans. New York: Paulist Press, 1987.

Biberian, Jerry, and Michael D. Whitty. *At Work: Spirituality Matters.* Scranton, Pa.: University of Scranton Press, 2007.

Bing, Stanley. *Sun Tzu Was a Sissy: Conquer Your Enemies, Promote Your Friends, and Wage the* Real *Art of War.* New York: HarperCollins, 2004.

Block, Peter. *Stewardship: Choosing Service over Self-Interest.* San Francisco: Berrett-Koehler, 1993.

Braganza, Abbot John, OSB. "The Monastery and the Seminary," *Pax Regis: Seminary of Christ the King* 1931-2006 66, no. 1 (December 2006): 1-6.

————. ed. *James, 1-2 Peter, 1-3 John, Jude,* Ancient Christian Commentary on Scripture, New Testament, vol. 11. Downers Grove, Ill: InterVarsity Press, 2000.

Bray, Gerald, ed. *Romans.* Ancient Christian Commentary on Scripture, New Testament, vol. 6. Downers Grove, Ill: InterVarsity Press, 1998.

Buechner, Frederick. *Wishful Thinking: A Seeker's ABC.* Rev. and expanded ed. San Francisco: HarperSanFrancisco, 1993.

Calvin, John. *Institutes of the Christian Religion.* Philadelphia: Westminster Press, 1960.

Carretto, Carlo. *Letters from the Desert.* Translated by Rose Mary Hancock. Maryknoll, N.Y.: Orbis Books, 2002.

Carter, Stephen L. *Integrity.* New York: Basic Books, 1996, quoted in David W. Gill, "No Integrity, No Trust; No Trust, No Business," *Ethix: The Bulletin of the Institute for Business, Technology, and Ethics* 14 (August 2000): 11.

Casey, Michael. *A Guide to Living in the Truth: Saint Benedict's Teaching on Humility.* Liguori, Mo.: Liguori, 2001.

Cassian, John. *The Conferences.* Translated by Boniface Ramsey. New York: Paulist Press, 1997.

————. *Conferences.* Translated by Colm Luibheid. New York: Paulist Press, 1985.

Chadwick, Owen. *John Cassian.* London: Cambridge University Press, 1968.

Congar, Yves. *Lay People in the Church: A Study for a Theology of the Laity.* Translated by D. Attwater. Westminster, Md.: Newman Press, 1957.

Conger, J., and others. *Spirit at Work: Discovering the Spirituality in Leadership.* San Franciso: Jossey-Bass, 1994.

Coombs, Ann. *The Living Workplace: Soul, Spirit, and Success in the 21st Century.* Toronto: HarperCollins, 2001.

Dale, Eric Steven. *Bringing Heaven Down to Earth: A Practical Spirituality of Work.* New York: Peter Lang, 1991.

Dalla Costa, John. *Magnificence at Work: Living Faith in Business.* Toronto: Novalis, 2005.

de Caussade, Jean-Pierre. *The Sacrament of the Present Moment.* Translated by Kitty Muggeridge. Glasgow: Silliam Collins and Co., 1987.

Delberg, Andre L. "Bridging the Gap Between Spirituality and Religion." In *Proceedings from the Santa Barbara Conference,* March 9-11, 2001.

de Sales, Francis. *Introduction to the Devout Life.* Translated and edited by John K. Ryan. New York: Image Books, 2003.

de Waal, Esther. *A Life-Giving Way: A Commentary on the Rule of St. Benedict.* Collegeville, Minn.: Liturgical Press, 1995.

Dielh, William E. *Thank God It's Monday.* Philadelphia: Fortress Press, 1982.

————. *The Monday Connection: A Spirituality of Competence, Affirmation, and Support in the Workplace.* San Francisco: HarperSanFrancisco, 1991.

Diehl, William E., and Judith R. Diehl. *It Ain't Over Till It's Over: A User's Guide to the Second Half of Life.* Minneapolis: Augsburg, 2003.

Drescher, John M. *Doing What Comes Spiritually.* Scottdale, Pa.: Herald Press, 1993.

Dreyer, Elizabeth A. *Earth Crammed with Heaven: A Spirituality of Everyday Life.* New York: Paulist Press, 1994.

Droel, William L. *Business People: The Spirituality of Work.* Chicago: ACTA Publications, 1990.

Fairlie, Henry. *The Seven Deadly Sins Today.* Notre Dame, Ind.: University of Notre Dame Press, 1979.

Fenelon, François. *The Royal Way of the Cross.* Edited by Hal Helms. Brewster, Mass.: Paraclete, 1982.

Flow, Donald E. "Profit." In *The Complete Book of Everyday Christianity,* edited by Robert Banks and R. Paul Stevens, pp. 809-13. Downers Grove, Ill.: InterVarsity Press, 1997.

Foster, Richard. *Money, Sex, and Power: The Challenge of the Disciplined Life.* San Francisco: Harper & Row, 1985.

Griffin, Emilie. *The Reflective Executive: A Spirituality of Business and Enterprise.* New York: Crossroad, 1993.

Hallowell, Edward M. "Overloaded Circuits: Why Smart People Underperform." In *Harvard Business Review on Bringing Your Whole Self to Work,* pp. 1-21. Boston: Harvard Business School Press, 2008.

Harmless, William. *Desert Christians: An Introduction to the Literature of Early Monasticism.* Oxford: Oxford University Press, 2004.

Haughey, John C. *Converting 9-5: A Spirituality of Daily Work.* New York: Crossroad, 1993.

Healy, S. D. *Boredom, Self, and Culture.* Cranbury, N.J.: Associate University Presses, 1984.

Heschel, Abraham. *The Sabbath: Its Meaning for Modern Man.* New York: Farrar, Straus and Giroux, 1951.

Hewlett, Sylvia Ann, and Carolyn Buck Luce. "Extreme Jobs: The Dangerous Allure of the 70-Hour Week." *Harvard Business Review* (December 2006): 49-59.

Hilton, Walter. *Toward a Perfect Love.* Translated by David Jeffrey. Portland, Oreg.: Multnomah Press, 1985.

Holland, Joe. *Creative Communion: Toward a Spirituality of Work.* New York: Crossroad, 1989.

Houston, James M. *Joyful Exiles: Life in Christ on the Dangerous Edge of Things.* Downers Grove, Ill.: InterVarsity Press, 2006.

Jarvik, Elaine. "Envy — Sin that's 'no fun at all' has elements of pride, greed, anger." *Deseret News.* http://www.deseretnews.com/article/1,5143,635197 503,00.html (accessed August 1, 2008).

Jordan-Smith, Paul. "Seven (and More) Deadly Sins." *Parabola* 10 (Winter 1985): 34-35.

Kass, Leon R. *The Hungry Soul: Eating and the Perfecting of Our Nature.* Chicago: University of Chicago Press, 1994.

Kidner, Derek. *The Proverbs: An Introduction and Commentary.* Chicago: InterVarsity Press, 1975.

———. *The Message of Ecclesiastes.* Downers Grove, Ill.: InterVarsity Press, 1976.

Kierkegaard, Søren. *Purity of Heart Is to Will One Thing.* New York: Harper & Brothers, 1948.

Klapp, O. E. *Overload and Boredom.* Westport, Conn.: Greenwood, 1986.

Lawrence, Brother. *The Practice of the Presence of God.* Grand Rapids: Spire, 1967.

Lechman, Judith C. *The Spirituality of Gentleness: Growing toward Christian Wholeness.* San Francisco: Harper and Row, 1987.

Leech, Kenneth. *True Prayer: An Invitation to Christian Spirituality.* San Francisco: Harper and Row, 1980.

Lewis, C. S. *Mere Christianity.* London: Geoffrey Bles, 1953.

Lowney, Chris. *Heroic Leadership: Best Practices from a 450-Year-Old Company That Changed the World.* Chicago: Loyola Press, 2003.

Lyman, Stanford M. *The Seven Deadly Sins and Evil.* Dix Hills, N.Y.: General Hall, Inc., 1989.

Marie-Eugene, P. *I Want to See God: A Practical Synthesis of Carmelite Spirituality.* Translated by M. Verda Clare. Notre Dame, Ind.: Christian Classics, 1953.

Matthew the Poor. *Orthodox Prayer Life: The Interior Way.* Crestwood, N. Y.: St. Vladimir's Seminary Press, 2003.

McCracken, Robert J. *What Is Sin? What Is Virtue?* New York: Harper and Row, 1966.

McMinn, Lisa G. *The Contented Soul: The Art of Savoring Life.* Downers Grove, Ill.: InterVarsity Press, 2006.

McNeill, Donald P., Douglas A. Morrison, and Henri J. M. Nouwen. *Compassion: A Reflection on the Christian Life.* Garden City, NY: Doubleday, 1982.

Meilaender, Gilbert C., ed. *Working: Its Meaning and Its Limits.* Notre Dame, Ind.: Notre Dame University Press, 2000.

————. "Mortality." *First Things* 10 (February 1991): 14-21.

Meisel, Anthony C., and M. L. del Mastro, trans. *The Rule of Saint Benedict.* New York: Doubleday, 1975.

Miller, Arthur. *Why You Can't Be Anything You Want to Be.* Grand Rapids: Zondervan, 1999.

Moltmann, Jürgen. *Theology of Hope: On the Ground and Implications of a Christian Eschatology.* Translated by James W. Leitch. New York: Harper and Row, 1967.

Muldoon, Tim. *The Ignatian Workout: Daily Spiritual Exercises for a Healthy Faith.* Chicago: Loyola Press, 2004.

Needleman, Jacob. *Money and the Meaning of Life.* New York: Doubleday, 1991.

Newbigin, Lesslie. *Honest Religion for Secular Man.* Philadelphia: Westminster Press, 1966.

————. *Foolishness to the Greeks: The Gospel and Western Culture.* Grand Rapids: Eerdmans, 1986.

Nouwen, Henri J. M. *In the Name of Jesus: Reflections on Christian Leadership.* New York: Crossroad, 1993.

Oates, W. E. "On Being a Workaholic." *Pastoral Psychology* 19 (October 1968): 16-20.

Olsson, Karl A. *Seven Sins and Seven Virtues.* New York: Harper and Brothers, 1962.

Palmer, Parker. *The Active Life: Wisdom for Work, Creativity, and Caring.* San Francisco: HarperSanFrancisco, 1990.

Pascal, Blaise. *Pensées.* Translated by A. J. Krailsheimer. London: Penguin Classics, 1995.

Pennington, M. Basil. *A School of Love: The Cistercian Way to Holiness.* Harrisburg, Pa.: Morehouse, 2000.

Perkins, William. *The Works of That Famous Minister of Christ in the University of Cambridge.* London: John Legatt, 1626.

Peterson, Eugene. "The Pastor's Sabbath." *Leadership* (Spring 1985): 52-58.

————. "Biblical Spirituality." Paper delivered to the faculty of Regent College, Vancouver, B.C., 1991.

————, and Anneke Kaai. *In a Word.* Brewster, Mass.: Paraclete, 2003.

Pierce, Gregory F. A. *Spirituality at Work: 10 Ways to Balance Your Life on the Job.* Chicago: Loyola Press, 2001.

Piper, John. "Battling the Unbelief of Lust." desiringGod http://www.desiringgod.org/ResourceLibrary/sermons/bydate/1988/657_Battling_the_Unbelief_of_Lust/ (accessed October 12, 2008).

Pollay, Richard, and R. Paul Stevens. "Advertising." In *The Complete Book of*

Everyday Christianity, edited by Robert Banks and R. Paul Stevens, pp. 23-27. Downers Grove, Ill.: InterVarsity Press, 1997.

Reed, Gerard. *C. S. Lewis Explores Vice and Virtue.* Kansas City: Beacon Hill Press, 2001.

Renesch, John, ed. *New Traditions in Business: Spirit and Leadership in the 21st Century.* San Francisco: Berrett-Koehler, 1992.

Rohr, Richard. "An Appetite for Wholeness." *Sojourners,* November 1982, p. 30.

Ruhlman, Michael. *Wooden Boats: In Pursuit of the Perfect Craft at an American Boatyard.* New York: Penguin Books, 2001.

Salkin, Jeffrey. *Being God's Partner: How to Find the Hidden Link Between Spirituality and Your Work.* Woodstock, Vt.: Jewish Lights, 1994.

Schein, Edgar H. *Organizational Culture and Leadership: A Dynamic View.* San Francisco: Jossey-Bass, 1991.

Schmemann, Alexander. *For the Life of the World: Sacraments and Orthodoxy.* Crestwood, N.Y.: St. Vladimir's Seminary Press, 1973.

Seerveld, Calvin. *Christian Workers, Unite!* Toronto: Christian Labour Association of Canada, 1964.

Silvoso, Ed. *Anointed for Business: How Christians Can Use Their Influence in the Marketplace to Change the World.* Ventura, Calif.: Regal, 2002.

Simetti, Manlio, ed. *Matthew 1–13.* Ancient Christian Commentary on Scripture, New Testament, vol. 1a. Downers Grove, Ill.: InterVarsity Press, 2001.

Singh, Sadhu Sundar. *With and Without Christ.* London: Cassell and Co., 1929.

"Some Sayings of the Desert Fathers." Villanova University. http://www 29.homepage.villanova.edu/christopher.haas/saying200f%20the %20desert%20fathers.html (accessed August 12, 2008).

Spidlik, Tomas. *The Spirituality of the Christian East: A Systematic Handbook.* Kalamazoo, Mich.: Cistercian Publications, 1986.

Stackhouse, Max, Dennis P. McCann, Shirley J. Roels, and Preston N. Williams, eds. *On Moral Business: Classical and Contemporary Resources for Ethics in Economic Life.* Grand Rapids: Eerdmans, 1995.

Stevens, R. Paul. "Boredom." In *The Complete Book of Everyday Christianity,* edited by Robert Banks and R. Paul Stevens, pp. 80-83. Downers Grove, Ill.: InterVarsity Press, 1997.

———. *Doing God's Business: Meaning and Motivation for the Marketplace.* Grand Rapids: Eerdmans, 2006.

———. "Drivenness." In *The Complete Book of Everyday Christianity,* edited by Robert Banks and R. Paul Stevens, pp. 312-18. Downers Grove, Ill.: InterVarsity Press, 1997.

————. *The Other Six Days: Vocation, Work, and Ministry in Biblical Perspective.* Grand Rapids: Eerdmans, 2000.

————. and Michael Green. *Living the Story: Biblical Spirituality for Everyday Christians.* Grand Rapids: Eerdmans, 2003.

————, and Robert Banks. *Marketplace Ministry Handbook.* Vancouver, B.C.: Regent College Publishing, 2005.

Strauch, Alexander. *Leading with Love.* Colorado Springs: Lewis and Roth, 2006.

Tabalujan, Benny. *God on Monday: Reflections on Christians @ Work.* Melbourne: Klesis Institute, 2005.

Teresa of Avila, *Interior Castle.* Translated by Allison Peers. New York: Doubleday, 1989.

Teresa, Mother. *No Greater Love.* Maryknoll, N.Y.: New World Library, 1997.

————. *Total Surrender.* Ann Arbor, Mich.: Servant Publications, 1985.

Terkel, Studs. *Working.* New York: Pantheon Books, 1972.

Thomas, Gary L. "Choosing gentleness: A gentle spirit gives the world a taste of the presence of Jesus." *Discipleship Journal* 18, no. 6 (Nov./Dec. 1998): 43-48.

Thurston, Bonnie. *Fruit of the Spirit: Growth of the Heart.* Collegeville, Minn.: The Liturgical Press, 2000.

Trump, Donald J. "The Fifth Deadly Workplace Sin: Sloth." The Trump Blog. Entry posted October 10, 2007. http://www.trumpuniversity.com/blog/post/2007/10/the-fifth-deadly-workplace-sin-sloth.cfm (accessed October 7, 2008).

————. "The Fourth Deadly Workplace Sin: Greed." The Trump Blog. Entry posted October 8, 2007. http://www.trumpuniversity.com/blog/post/2007/10/the-fourth-deadly-workplace-sin-greed.cfm (accessed October 12, 2008).

Tuohy, Wendy. "Love in a corporate climate." The Age. http://www.theage.com.au/articles/2003/07/25/1059084206429.html (accessed September 3, 2008).

Underhill, Evelyn. *The Fruits of the Spirit.* Wilton, Conn.: Morehouse-Barlow Co., 1981.

Ung, Alvin. "Passions and Purity: Seeking a Pure Heart through Ministry and Spirituality." *Crux* 41, no. 2 (Summer 2005): 3-32.

Van Kaam, Adrian. *Spirituality and the Gentle Life.* Dentville, N.J.: Dimension Books, 1974.

Vanier, Jean. *Community and Growth.* Translated by Jean Vanier. New York: Paulist Press, 1989.

Vest, Norvene. *Friend of the Soul: A Benedictine Spirituality of Work.* Cambridge, Mass.: Cowley Publications, 1997.

Volf, Miroslav. *Work in the Spirit: Toward a Theology of Work.* New York: Oxford University Press, 1991.

von Speyr, Adrienne. *The Discourses of Controversy: Meditations on John 6–12.* Translated by Brian McNeil. San Francisco: Ignatius, 1993.

Waldrop, M. Mitchell. "Dee Hock on Management: Dee Hock's management principles, in his own words." *Fast Company* 5 (October 1996): 79.

Ward, Benedicta, SLG, trans. *The Sayings of the Desert Fathers: The Alphabetical Collection.* London: Cistercian Publications, 1985.

Wesley, John. "The Use of Money." In *On Moral Business: Classical and Contemporary Resources for Ethics in Economic Life,* edited by Max L. Stackhouse, Dennis P. McCann, Shirley J. Roels, and Preston N. Williams, pp. 194-97. Grand Rapids: Eerdmans, 1995.

"Who me, unbalanced?: A 5-minute quiz that will reveal the truth." *The Office Journal* 3, no. 4 (June & July 2006): 12, http://www.makeitbusiness.com/downloads/BackIssues/June%20&%20July%202006.pdf (accessed August 12, 2008).

Willard, Dallas. *Renovation of the Heart.* Colorado Springs: Navpress, 2002.

Willimon, William H. *Sinning Like a Christian: A New Look at the Seven Deadly Sins.* Nashville: Abingdon Press, 2005.

Wilson, Rod. "Shabbat and Shalom." *The Regent World* 20, no. 2 (Winter 2008): 1.

Winter, Bruce. *Seek the Welfare of the City: Christians as Benefactors and Citizens.* Grand Rapids: Eerdmans, 1994.

"Work-life balance." Wikipedia. http://en.wikipedia.org/wiki/Work_life_balance (accessed October 9, 2008).

Wright, Clive. *The Business of Virtue.* London: SPCK, 2004.

Wright, N. T. *The Challenge of Jesus: Rediscovering Who Jesus Was and Is.* Downers Grove, Ill.: InterVarsity Press, 1999.

Wyszyński, Stefan Cardinal. *All You Who Labor: Work and the Sanctification of Daily Life.* Manchester, N.H.: Sophia Institute Press, 1995.

Younger, K. Lawson, Jr. *Judges, Ruth.* In The NIV Application Commentary. Grand Rapids: Zondervan, 2002.

Index of Authors

Index of Subjects

Index of Scripture References